PLAYING *by the* UNWRITTEN RULES III
Here is What I Think: This is What I Know

Katharine,

May this book answer questions you have yet to ask!

Dr. [signature]
3/2020

PLAYING *by the* UNWRITTEN RULES III
Here is What I Think: This is What I Know

DR. INDIGO DEBRA TRIPLETT

PLAYING *by the* UNWRITTEN RULES III

Here is What I Think: This is What I Know
By Dr. Indigo Debra Triplett

indigo@4-DPerformance.com
www.4-DPerformance.com

All rights reserved. No part of this book may be copied, reproduced, transcribed, transmitted or distributed in any form by any means— electronic, mechanical, data base or any information retrieval system— except for brief quotations or review by media, radio or television without written permission from the publisher. Quotations from this book may not be used without reference.

The pieces of information in this book were obtained from the author's research, personal experiences and insights. While every effort has been made to make this book as accurate as possible, the author disclaims any liability or risk as a direct or indirect consequence of the use of the contents of this book.

ISBN 978-0-9843491-2-8

Copyright © 2019, 4D Performance Ltd., All Rights Reserved.

Contents

About the Author vi

Dedication viii

Introduction ix

1. The Difficulty in Life is the Choices 1

2. Uncommon Unwritten Rules 18

3. Resilience: Weathering Your Storm 42

4. Forgiveness and Letting Go: A Game Changer 61

5. The Practicality of Spirituality 98

6. Indigoisms for Insight 117

About the Author

Dr. Indigo has over 20 years of experience in successfully owning and operating a business in the US. She launched 4D Performance Sdn. Bhd., in Malaysia in 2017. She was featured in Inc. Magazine, Fox News, New York Times, Huffington Post, and many other media outlets that took notice of her ability to grow a home-based business into a thriving enterprise. She has earned many accolades and awards such as a Trail Blazer Award and more, but what she is most proud of is that her company, Careers In Transition, Inc., was listed on the Inc. Magazine Top 500 Fastest Growing Companies in America, in 2012 and 2013. Under her leadership, her company held contracts ranging from 1.5 million to a single contract valued at 18 million dollars. Aside from leading her company, she helps organizations grow through talent management and compete on the glocal (global/local) market based on her international experience and research. Dr. Indigo earned a Ph.D. in Values-Driven Leadership, which she utilizes to help decision makers and leaders become more effective in the workplace and she introduced, in Asia, a new philosophy on developing employees to enhance performance. Her expertise and philosophy were garnered from working with organizations such as NASA, Environmental Protection Agency, Office of Personnel Management, Central Intelligence Agency, Time Warner, Pentagon, US Army, Army Corps of Engineers, Homeland Security, Federal Aviation Administration, Transportation Security Administration, FBI, Governmental Accountability Office, Centers for Disease Control and Prevention, Department of State, Millennium Challenge Corporation, Federal Reserve Board, USAID, Veterans Affairs Administration, Turner Broadcasting, Halliburton, Delta Airlines, WHSmith, LexisNexis Risk Solutions, Sodexo, DeVry University, Emory University, George Washington University, Spelman College, Gwinnet College and more.

Her passion is providing transformational insight. Her unique programs allow people to recalibrate, rebuild, refocus, and reenergize while receiving *insight* in a safe space to be transparent and authentic. Her programs are grounded in 25 years of best practices around career development and career management steeped in purpose and passion. Her services are a coaching relationship for some, and a respite for others. Through a variety of transformational techniques, clients are surrounded with support and guidance. According to Dr. Indigo, her commitment and goal is to offer services that help people become career resilient by tapping into their uniqueness and strengths to develop their best self.

Dr. Indigo's international career journey through Asia began in 1983, as a young service member in the United States Marine Corps while stationed in Okinawa, Japan. She served as a representative under USDA Graduate School's umbrella; whereby, she presented to 25 Chinese delegates visiting the US to learn about HR practices. Then in 2012 she returned to Asia for her Ph.D. internship in Beijing, China. After sharing the first two books in the series *Playing by the Unwritten Rules* with an HR leader, she was asked to speak to HR managers at a symposium in Beijing, and then invited to Shanghai, China, by the University of Hong Kong to speak to its alumni and HR students. That was the beginning of what became a part of her calling to relocate to Asia, in 2016.

Based on her US and international experience and expertise in helping companies to attract, develop and retain employees, she supports Asian organizations in becoming more competitive to contribute to the economic growth that is predicted. It is her sincere desire to help contribute to the economic growth and be a part of Asia's success by infusing her diverse knowledge, skills and abilities into Asia. Her passion is speaking on transformation, spirituality and mental wellness. She has spoken at Google-Singapore, International SOS, Asian Strategy & Leadership Institute (ASLI), P&G, Singapore International Chamber of Commerce, Icon, British Malaysia Chamber of Commerce, Petrofac, PrimeTime-Singapore, University of Hong Kong, Abbott, Philippine HR Congress, Singapore Management University and other organizations throughout Asia. She is picking up momentum in Asia and has been featured in *High Net Worth* online publication, in Singapore and in *FEMINA*, one of Indonesia's oldest and largest women's magazine. She is also a collaborator in a book titled, *SPEAK-the Women's Guide to Public Speaking and Changing the World*. She authored the chapter titled, "The Dollars and Sense of Speaking Professionally."

Dedication

This book is dedicated to all my clients who have supported me since I branched out as an entrepreneur in 1995. You've allowed me to grow both personally and professionally with you as a client. Thank you for granting me access to your organization, which became a space for learning and experimenting. What I offered and refined over the years was based on my being able to move about in your organization and interact with employees at all levels and tiers. What I know was not discovered in a textbook, but rather through application based on your willingness to work with me on going into uncharted areas. Then, there is a special client whom I want to thank. He gave more to me than I gave to him, which is not the norm in most vendor client relationships. William G. Bostic, Jr. (Bill), who retired as former Associate Director for Economic Programs for the U.S. Census Bureau, was more than just a client. He was an advocate. He believed in me and my products so much so that he purchased 1,000 copies of both books in the series, *Playing by the Unwritten Rules* which makes mentioning him not required but essential. Then he trusted my products enough to allow me to work on a change management initiative that catapulted my company onto a wider and bigger stage. And, he did all this with complete respect for me and valued me as a business owner. He was the perfect gentleman. There were numerous other clients who were also advocates, mentors and colleagues, and for that I want to thank them without this becoming an Oscar speech.

And the award for best supporting ensemble goes to many of my employees and colleagues over the years. In particular, I want to thank Nona Richardson, Chief Strategist of MitchRich Communications who was at first a client, then an employee, and now she's a vendor. She edited this book. Through each of our job stages together, we remained career friends and sistahs. She has been here for me in so many ways and I pray that she can say the same for me. I absolutely respect, admire and love that girl.

I cannot end this series without thanking my three sons, Russell David Johnson, who inspired me on many levels, and Austin Sinclair and Hunter Tale Johnson, who came with me to Asia. Our lives have been so enriched by the experience of being global citizens. Thank you for taking this amazing journey with me. And, most of all, you helped me to want to live again. For that I am deeply grateful to have you in my life.

Introduction

This is the 3rd installment of a three-part series *Playing by the Unwritten Rules*. The first book was *Moving from the Middle to the Top* and the second book was *From a Job Defense to a Career Offense*. I am so thrilled about this book *Here is What I Think: This is What I Know* because it brings closure to a chapter in my life/career and to the *Playing by the Unwritten Rules* series. Countless numbers of these books have been sold around the world. I'm proud of each book, but this book is taking career success to a whole new level! I'm so excited about this book that if I had a tail it would be wagging like a puppy who has received a fresh new bone.

Here is some context on what to expect. I was in Phuket, in Thailand, Batam and Bintan, in Indonesia and the Philippines, writing on the beach to complete this book. For each of the previous books in this series, I would travel to a nice location, preferably by water, to be inspired. I thought that I 'needed' to reconstruct the environment that I created for each of the previous books. I would listen to jazz from sun up to sun down, writing nonstop, except to eat and occasionally stretch. I felt that I needed to recreate what made me successful. But, I have realized that I don't have to continue doing the same things for success. Yes, it is true that certain things set the tone for a writer's creative juices to flow, but what I'm writing about is less creative and more reflective. What I've come to see is that my two books about career success were more about the "what" and now I'm writing about the "how." So, I don't need to be in a charming hotel or time share condo doing some of the ritualistic things that I required initially. But, I do want an ocean and the waves, which provide a tranquil setting for me to stay in a positive space when my thoughts take me to some of the harsh realities that I've encountered, in the last few years. An ocean? I don't need it, but rather I want it. I'm wearing the same pink t-shirt that I wore whenever I wrote, but I don't need it, but rather I want it because it makes me feel good. It's a T-shirt with a cartoon picture of a woman saying, "I know I'm in my own little world, but it's ok, they know me here." And, I have a coffee cup that I travel with to write, with the exact same picture, slogan and color as my T-shirt. I've been on the beach either outside my 'glamping' tent or in a cabin typing and loving it. My son said to me that what I am doing is not work, as he was attempting to justify why he didn't need to work while I was out of the office. I argued that writing is in fact work. In fact, I was offended that he even implied that what I'm doing is merely having fun. He then retorted that the saying goes, "When you love what you do, you never work a day in your life." Ouch… he's right: that's true. But, it is still work even if it is fun, I pointed out! It is work because I have to go deep into some files buried deep in my mind to give you context about the game. I have to tap into some negative thoughts about situations that I thought would kill me, but rather have made me stronger, to share with you how to forgive, let go and move on. Also, I have to be authentic, honest and transparent, which, when combined, is not a natural space to be for people in general. I must open myself to you so that you can stand on my shoulders, which I believe will help you attain new heights. Lastly, I must humble myself to tell my story and my truth so that you can understand how to do some of the most difficult things in life that have no instructional guide, playbook or recipe. So, this is work and this is life. And, life is an excellent teacher: she gives you the test first and then teaches you the lesson. I hope this book serves as a cliff note or cheat sheet for your future success. I saw this saying, "Sometimes my life feels like a pop quiz that I didn't study for." If you ever feel this way, this book is certainly for you.

I said all that to say this: change and transformation are life's most precious journey. A life lesson that I had is that I cannot and should not do things the exact same way because I'm no longer the woman, business owner, professional, mother, etc. who wrote the last two books over a 13-year period. There is absolutely nothing that I would change in the other two books. I said what I meant and meant what I said. But, I am no longer the same person who wrote those books. I have new ideas, new experiences and a completely altered life and career journey that I never anticipated. I'm also much older and near retirement, so what I value in life and expect from a career is far different from where I was in 2005. That is the natural order of things and life's progression that I bring to you. Growth is about change, and success comes with transformation. However, the game has not changed. Yes, there are different players but, the needle hasn't moved. Companies, organizations, and decision-makers are still playing the game and expecting that you know and understand the unwritten rules. What I want to do is to collect all the knowledge that I garnered over the years to add to the information that I've already shared with you through the two previous books.

I am much older with many stories and experiences under my belt to share. I will be writing about things that I witnessed and experienced over the years. I often say that life is a rollercoaster. Life has the ups, downs, twists and turns. You are either riding the rollercoaster with your hands in the air enjoying all that it brings or holding on to the bar tightly across your lap or chest, wishing the ride will end or that it will continue for another lap. Life and your career are merely about choices, regardless of how you experience the ride. This book may at times even sound like a journal because I will pull things from my personal journal for accuracy. I'll explain the importance of a journal in the first chapter.

I'll also give an international perspective, since I now live in Asia after a series of events that brought me here. I was both pulled and pushed into Asia which I will speak about in subsequent chapters. Often a job description will state that you must have at a minimum two years of demonstrable experience. Well, with my work with the Army Corps of Engineers in Germany, my internship in Beijing, China to work on my Ph.D. and working throughout South East Asia, for now, I believe that I can speak of 'the game' as an international/global citizen and career professional. Although, I had no intentions on starting a new career in Asia, at my age, I have acquired continued success because I understand and will play the game.

And, let me address this age thing. People like to say that age is nothing but a number. That's poppy cock; just ask a highly educated millennial seeking to gain experience but her boss keeps making her *sit the bench* because she hasn't put in her proverbial time. Or, look at the Walmart greeter who was put out to pasture somewhere and has decided to work anywhere to simply keep busy and connected to the real world. Well, maybe not him, but I do know of a company that requires its employees to retire at a certain age. I was shocked when a would-be client said that he was retiring just as he was trying to bring me into the company. We went out for coffee and he shared that he didn't want to leave but the company had a long-standing policy that he had to adhere to. That really sucked. But, the case in point is that ageism is probably more prevalent and just as insidious as any other ism. So, I will honor the fact that I'm older but face the reality that age plays a significant role in my success and sometimes difficulties in moving into new areas. So, don't get hung up when I vent that I'm too old for this crap at some point: I'm just stating my reality.

So, back to the point. In essence, I will bring closure to some past chapters, so if you haven't read the first two books it would be time well-spent doing so. For instance, in the second book I spent time discussing ageism in a chapter devoted to diversity. I gave suggestions on how to attain success as a young professional and as a seasoned professional faced with ageism. These books will give you insight and context to what I am saying. However, this book, similar to the other two books is a stand-alone book. I'm only recommending that you read the first two books, but it is by no means required for understanding the messages in this book.

If you are not sure what this book series is truly about, it is quite simple: I want this book to be a guide and source to creating a career resilient workforce whether I am here in Asia, traveling the world or living in America. I see myself as a global citizen. I think that the success of all countries is their contribution to the glocal (global/local) economy which is good for all humanity. This means the global workforce must have career management and career development for career resilience:

> By a career resilient workforce, we mean: "A group of employees, who not only are dedicated to the idea of continuous learning but also stand ready to reinvent themselves to keep up with change; who take responsibility for their own career management, and last but not least, who are committed to the company's success."
>
> -- J.H. Waterman, R.H. Waterman, B.A. Collard,
> Harvard Business Review

I have had many years to build a business, work with people around the world and enjoy life to the fullest. However, I have experienced things in life that I could not have fathomed. I think people look for books to tell them things that will help them to make barrels and barrels of money. But, as I am turning the corner on my career and have made barrels and barrels of money, I've discovered that there are some things that no one talks about. People don't discuss the stuff that happens in the workplace that ultimately impacts your life. This book is unique, being that I'm going to talk to you about things that most people would not disclose because it is really the secret to success. Yes, playing the game is required but it's how you play the game which will have a long-lasting impact. It's how you respond to the ups and downs in your career and how you treat people, in general. I'm elated about this final book in this series. I'm leaving nothing on the table when it comes to the *unwritten rules*.

This book will be best read when you are in a quiet space where you can reflect, take notes and sip a glass of wine or two; I'm just saying. But, if that isn't your thing...then pour a cup of tea or coffee and fasten your seat belt. The chapters are following a path, i.e. the "Introduction" is just creating a space for us to meet up; "The Difficulty in Life is the Choices" is setting the tone and foundation of the book; "Uncommon Unwritten Rules" is sharing with you what you should know merely as a basis for playing the game; then I move into "Resilience: Weathering Your Storm" which seems to be missing in many people's lives and career. I can see all across the world that things are changing and not necessarily for the better. We need to teach resiliency in classes for children all the way to business schools for leaders. Next, I have "Forgiveness and Letting Go: A Game Changer" which is about forgiveness and letting go. There are two skills and abilities to harness that everyone advocates but no one ever tells us how to do it. Then I open my heart to you with what has helped me in this crazy world and within a business climate that can be harsh and not for the faint at heart. I added "The Practicality of Spirituality" because we don't typically hear about it in business books and it's often confused with religion. I finish with "Indigoisms for Insight" which are my anectdotal perspectives.

Each of these chapters is rich and grounded in both research and experience. I believe your life will be changed upon reading each chapter by taking notes and rereading when somethng doesn't seem to make sense. Don't make the mistake of not reading one or the other chapters because of your preconcieved notions or views. I'll also repeat myself from chapter to chapter to make sure you understand what I am conveying. I may say the same thing but slightly dissimilar for a different perspective in that chapter. Ironically, there are things that we never hear about so they need repeating for understanding. Spaced repetition is how Americans learn things such as our alphabets and multiplication tables. I will use a slight variance to spaced repetiton. I will use the 'mother' way of communicating which is to say something over and over until she thinks that you got it, and then she'll think you need reminding so she will tell you the same thing again. But, all in all, these chapters flow and come together to give you a ring side seat to my career, told with complete love and insight to support you on your journey and future circumstances. May this book answer questions you have yet to ask.

Chapter 1

The Difficulty in Life is the Choices

The first two books of this three-part series focused on two areas: career management and career development. I spent an inordinate amount of time bringing about an awareness about "the game." I don't believe the existence of the game is debatable. At this point, I am finding that people generally accept that a game is being played. Now, it is a matter of whether professionals are willing to play or not, so they think. There are some whom I've met who will say that they did not or do not play the game, but when I ask questions about their success and/or career journey, they begin to nod their head in agreement that they do in fact do certain things, whether consciously or unconsciously. These things can be as easy as influencing others through their knowledge or personal charisma. It can be just having a relationship with their boss that allows their boss to feel supported and respected. At the end of the day, let's face it…there are three things that people want regardless of where they live in the world, where they sit in the organization or their role and responsibility, personally and professionally. People want to be valued, respected, and understood. And, when you do those things, you are well on your way to mastering the game. You may be thinking that such is not playing the game. You may further think that such is just being nice, courteous or genuine. Playing the game doesn't mean not being genuine, etc. In fact, a true game player will be these things because it fosters healthy relationships. I can't emphasize this enough: the game is not a bad thing…it simply is the culture of an organization. But, let me be clear that there is a game that has both written and unwritten rules. Either you are on a full court press or sitting the bench, but you are playing the game by merely showing up.

Whether you work in a religious institution, higher education, non-profit, Non-Government Organization (NGO), Small to Medium Enterprise (SME) or corporation; there is a game, yeah. In essence, the game is the informal culture that shapes the organization and guides behavior. As I have been saying for years, every professional company should have an employee handbook of some sort, which usually informs employees of their rights and responsibilities. Although, that is not a hard and fast rule or fact. Now, with that being said…an employee handbook which are written rules to the game merely helps an employee keep his job while the unwritten rules help you to become promotable.

I've been at this thing for over 25 years, watching careers, coaching executives and being privy to information kept close to the chest of powerful people. I have had and continue to have a seat at the table where decisions are made, and I can see the game being played out every day. Don't kill the messenger, but it's not how hard you work, it's not how smart you are or even how much money you make for the company (although that is a plus); it's how much people either like or dislike you, and it's how much you are seen as a player on the team regardless of title, tenure or rank. If there is a team and you are a player, in short, there is a game. I'm spending time attempting to prove something that I know exists and thousands of others have acknowledged to make sure we are all on the same page before I share myself, my thoughts and my spirit with you. I need you to know that this is coming from a place of love. The first two books were more about awareness while this book is the how on playing the game.

Several years ago, I was speaking at the US Government Accountability Office. Before I spoke, there was much debate about the validity of the subject. And, approval on my presentation was sought from leadership because the topic could be seen as controversial. However, the organization had an independent audit conducted and it clearly stated that diversity was an issue and that the unwritten rules were not understood. That was amazing because GAO is an independent, nonpartisan agency that works for Congress. It is often called the "congressional watchdog," that I believe holds my government accountable to upholding integrity, ethics, etc. But, what is more interesting is that at that time and for many years, GAO has been ranked as one of the best places to work. So, I was (1) very honored to speak at an all hands forum in their auditorium. And, (2) I was very intrigued by the audit that quoted how the unwritten rules were not understood which led to a perceivable diversity issue. They had people from every level and tier there; especially leadership, in case something went awry. I was hired to speak about the unwritten rules based on the audit results. My presentation was the normal discussion that included audience participation and exploring existing unwritten rules within the organization while in a safe environment. I know. You are probably wondering how safe can it be with a few hundred people. Yes…it was safe. There is a technique that I use to allow transparency and disclosure without risk. So, everyone was involved, engaged and having fun while learning, right? Immediately, after my presentation, people created a line to say thank you, buy my books and/or express their appreciation, especially leadership who ordinarily cannot speak about the unwritten rules or the game, for a variety of reasons as mentioned in the second book. As the line dwindled and people started leaving, I was packing up to go when a Hispanic guy approached me. I saw him milling around but thought nothing of it because some people want to speak to me in privacy about situations they are encountering that they want to keep confidential. But, not this guy. He was angry. First, he expressed that he was annoyed that I didn't like men. I looked puzzled and asked why he would draw that conclusion. He said that I proudly said that I have placed men on pause. I smiled and asked if he remembered the context when I made that reference. He didn't (sigh). His brain had shut off when he heard something that made him feel uncomfortable. I reminded him that because I was getting older, I can't always rely on my memory. And since I had forgotten a phrase, I said, "Some of you ladies know exactly what I'm talking about when you are over 50. You are putting men-on-pause." It was a play on words for menopause; whereby, women have memory problems, hot sweats and a host of other crap that someone else can write about. So, I smiled and explained that to him and he was obviously embarrassed about not getting the joke or reacting so emotionally.

I explained that I try to connect with all people on various levels. I tell jokes that men would appreciate, stories that managers would value, and so forth. I may not be able to get everyone in my boat, but I want to make sure no one is on the dock punching holes in my boat. I have to make my message palatable. But, that was only the start: he wasn't finished. His next complaint was that I, as a black woman, should be ashamed of myself for telling people of color to play the game. Huh? …. Very interesting. I never thought about it and maybe others have felt the same way. I shared with him that I don't agree with the game and I didn't create the game, but I'm a messenger. I only share with people how to have freedom and success. Shame on me to know how someone can improve upon his life and career but not tell him, right? To tell people to not play the game is counterproductive and will not serve them well. But more importantly, you have choices. The difficulty in life is choices. You can choose how to play or how not to play, although by the very nature of employment or contractual relationships, you are in a game. I just provide you with the information to make a choice and the choice is yours. I don't always like having to play the damn game all the damn time, but if I want certain perks and benefits in my career, I must play the game and play to win; just like everyone else. No one is exempt. His agitated response reminded me of why I do this.

Think of it like this, if you think you are not in the game. If you are on the playground as a child and children are playing tag. Someone may run up to you, tap you and yell, "Tag! You are it." You can cross your arms, and say, "I'm not playing!" No one cares. You just lost. And, if you walk off the playground, you merely look like a sore loser. It's stupid, but it's the unwritten rules of the playground at that very moment, and everyone is playing the game. You can decide to not fit in or be the square peg, if you choose to, but there are consequences. As for the guy, he expressed an appreciation for my taking time to share some inner thoughts with him that I didn't disclose on the stage. Before completely packing up, I think he bought the books. No, I'm sure he bought a book, come to think of it. And, get this. We stayed in touch for a while. I think he thought it was his appointed duty to keep me on my toes.

Now, here is something I want to share with you about freedom. I often liken myself to Harriet Tubman who was a Black abolitionist who helped many American slaves escape to freedom. I believe that I help people escape from self-bondage or career bondage placed on them by society, corporate rules, self, etc. To successfully play the game gives you some level of freedom or at a minimum a pathway to success that leads to freedom. However, some view the game or playing the game as limiting and controlling. But, it boils down to situational judgment and knowing when and how to respond to different things at the appropriate time. Therefore, some people have misperceptions about the game and refuse to play by the unwritten rules.

During one of Harriet Tubman's interviews, she was asked about how she felt freeing or leading thousands to freedom and her response was, "I could have led a thousand more, if only they knew they were slaves." In my line of work, some people have no idea that they are not free. And, some people have been beaten down for so long that they begin to think that it's normal. I speak of having a career where you can express yourself through your work and that is freedom. If you recall the Hispanic guy who was angry with me about sharing that minorities needed to play the game, he was like many blacks who were slaves and refused to escape.

Some professionals don't even recognize that they are slaves to poor habits, horrible bosses, jobs that prevent work life balance, etc. Many slaves stayed on those plantations for many reasons, ranging from fear of death and torture if caught to believing that things would be no better, or even worse if they left. Does this sound familiar with how and why people stay in relationships or jobs far too long? Harriet had to risk everything for some who would have betrayed her, but she continued to lead people to freedom. I have people who cannot understand what I do or why I do it. But, there are the few who totally get it and will allow me to guide them to freedom. Freedom could be to become an entrepreneur, receive a promotion from a dead-end job, or just gain some peace of mind. I hope that this book gives you the courage to be free, the ability to seek freedom and the roadmap to inner peace.

So, the next few chapters will explore the things I do to play the game with integrity, which has led to my personal and professional success. I will also share with you a four-year storm that nearly took my life twice, to be completely transparent. No one, not even I, can have everything go well all of the time. This is going to be a tough book to write because I will be completely vulnerable with candor in hopes that it will help you in your journey.

Let's talk a little more about choices. I had a coffee cup that stated, "The difficulties in life are not the problems but the choices." I think the problem with people not embracing or understanding the game is that they don't believe that they have a choice. You are making a choice whether you are an active player or sitting the bench. You may want to read the first chapter of my first book for this information. But, as a slight continuation, you must know that you have a choice. When your boss or even your peers ask you to join them after work for drinks or to drop by their house for a cookout on the weekend, and you decide that you will only deal with them during work hours, that is a choice. When you decide not to sit on some information during a meeting and tell your boss that her figures are skewed or tell your peer that they have faulty thinking in front of others, those certainly are choices.

An unwritten rule is never to embarrass your boss, or your peer for that matter. There are other ways of handling all these situations, but you can choose to "do you." That expression is so urban, but it speaks to the heart of everything. DO YOU. I have to laugh when I say to friends, "I'm doing me." During the holidays, I don't get properly dressed, don't put on deodorant, don't fix my hair or do anything. I'm just doing me. A me who doesn't give a darn about anything except getting my rest and unplugging. Yet, I understand that I don't have the luxury of doing me when I am in business mode. It feels so good to do me, but a client doesn't pay for me to do me, and an employer doesn't pay you to do you, whatever you may be. I often say that employers hire people for what they can do and fire you for who you are. Unfortunately, organizations are not designed for everyone to be their whole self. That is a harsh reality.

A friend and colleague who is a successful black woman attorney from London working in the shipping industry struggles with the identity that she wants to project versus what she has to project. Our conversations always seem to center on our hair. We can talk about work, relationships, and things in general, but the conversation always touches upon hair. That's right, something as simple and meaningless as hair. Many black women struggle with the hair thing. Black professionals have to strike a balance of being true to ourselves while not appearing too ethnic. Now some will read this and say, "that is absolutely not true." However, I assure you that if you ask a black professional woman about the hair situation you will have an entirely different conversation, if she is able to speak with truth and candor. If we wear braids, locks or a natural, we can be perceived as too ethnic and cause some people to feel uncomfortable. So, we often opt for wigs, relaxers, extensions, weaves and many other styles that are costly and well, unsafe and unhealthy.

Now, back to the attorney. At one time, she wore a relaxed (chemically altered process), short and sassy style. She went back to Europe and had micro braids put in. They were adorable! Then, she explained to me that when she went to work everyone asked about her braids. No one said they were nice but rather there were questions upon questions. She told them that she changed her style for the holidays but that wasn't the truth. She wanted the style as an everyday look. Her boss's wife even called her and asked about the braids and said that her husband couldn't explain the look, which demonstrated that her looks made it to the dining room table. She had a choice to make. Either keep the ethnic look that I love, and think is adorable, or choose a style that is considered more "professional." Your looks should never cause your skills to be in the shadow. I can't believe I'm still talking about this issue in today's global market.

Hell, in 1995, I was called Buckwheat, an iconic stereotype character from the children's show *Little Rascals*. It stemmed from me changing from a "professional" look to wearing my hair natural. I tell this story in the second book within the diversity chapter. So, I'll give a synopsis. I was hired for what I could offer and when I changed my looks, which made people uncomfortable, I was fired. This is a fact, this is real, and it was damaging to my self-esteem and self-worth. My previous boss shared with me that I didn't give them a chance to know me before going all ethnic on my new colleagues. I had a choice. I could keep the new natural look or go back to the long relaxed look. I decided to be me. I found a look that I could embrace while playing the diversity game. That pushed me out of corporate America and pulled me into entrepreneurship. I started my own business and wore a short style that helped minimize sexual harassment (another story for another time) while appearing polished and professional. It's not fair but it's a stupid reality that you can either ignore and be you, or chose to deal with it until you are in a position to change up the rules of the game. As long as I have clients, the game will exist for me and as long as you have anyone signing your check, there will be a game imposed.

Changing my hairstyle doesn't make me lose sleep at night. My colleague not wearing braids as an attorney in an ultra-conservative male environment doesn't cause her to feel slighted. It's just a part of the game. There are many rules that companies have that you must abide by. It's just that the unwritten rules are often unfair, biased and so forth. You should ask yourself whether what is being expected of you goes against the grain or is it just your personal preference that is causing you to push back. Hair is a personal preference for you and a professional preference for those around you, e.g. boss, peers, leadership, etc. If my hair is going to be so disruptive or cause people to not see me, then I'm willing to wear a style that we all can live with. I know that sucks, right? With that being said, what is most important is to never play the game by rules that run counter to your beliefs, integrity and so forth.

Some rules are blatant while others are so subtle that you abide by them and don't even realize it, such as body piercing and tattoos. In some environments, it is quite alright to have both to any extent you choose. But, let's take a sample profession. Would you trust or feel comfortable with an attorney who you interview to take your case who is wickedly smart, but he has a nose ring and/or face tattoo. Let's just say that you are being charged with something that can land you or your child some jail time, i.e. prison sentence if found guilty. You may still say yes. It doesn't matter how he looks, if he can win the case is what you are thinking. But, here's the problem: there will be several jurors who will make judgements about his character and possibly not hear anything he has to say on your behalf. While you are open and accepting, others may not be, which is how perception impacts us. You may never know that three people on the jury are offended by his looks, which will impact your chances of a fair trial. Do you want that? No…but that is life and reality. We cannot totally control how people perceive us, but we don't have to fuel their biases.

We can do what is within our control to manage people's perception to an extent. So, I don't wear a natural hair style based on past prejudices and recent encounters that my peers have also experienced. My attorney friend had other black professionals give her push back about changing her hairstyle. I asked her to consider whether the people advising her to keep her micro braids are in prominent positions such as her career track or even on a career trajectory that exceeds her. Hands down they weren't. Be careful of people who tell you that you don't have to play the game or to 'do you' when they are not in a position that gives them access to how decision-makers think. They don't know what they don't know.

It's very disheartening that we have to make choices. But, such is life. And, I would be misleading you if I told you that it gets easier the higher you go. The game still exists but with diverse players and different rules. And the game isn't so intrusive as how you wear your hair. It can be simple things such as coming in early and leaving late to appease your boss. It can be anything from the easy peasy stuff to complicated matters attached to egos. Some things will come naturally while other things may give you pause. Then there are rules that may seem totally out in left field such as 'don't have nicer clubs than your boss when golfing with him'. Men often joke about that silly rule but adhere to it when their career mobility or success is closely reliant on their boss who they 'must' golf with on a regular basis. That is not something that I concern myself with as a golfer, but I can certainly understand their plight. This is something they have to contend with, which goes to say, just because a rule doesn't impact you doesn't mean it doesn't exist or isn't a dilemma for someone else.

As we move through this book, you will need to make some choices on how you will deal with the information. Some things you may find off putting because they may prick a nerve. You may find some things silly because you cannot identify with them. You may read something that you totally agree with or find irrelevant. I suggest that you take what works for you and toss away what doesn't work, or park it in the back of your mind for later use. If there is something that invokes an emotion of sadness, anger, etc. explore why that is bothering you so that you can deal with it appropriately. Don't discount it: there's a reason it is nagging at you.

It all boils down to self-management. Self-management is a combination of self-awareness, self-knowledge, and self-acceptance. All three of these must intersect for self-management. You cannot play the game effectively if you cannot manage yourself. This doesn't mean not having feelings associated with something, but rather understanding these feelings. In any given situation, you must be aware of something, e.g. a person's tone, the way a person speaks, their idiosyncrasies, what is said, etc. These things can impact or trigger something in you. For example, if you become agitated about something, you are aware. However, there are instances you are agitated and don't even know it until someone asks you whether something is wrong. It is not uncommon for someone to be agitated and act out in such a way that causes everyone around them to know something is wrong, and even when told that they are either mad, agitated or something, they will deny it because they aren't self-aware. So, self-awareness is huge. It's the beginning of changing behaviors or improving yourself.

Self-awareness is simply the knowing about something. Then comes the self-knowledge. That is distinct from self-awareness. It is knowing the 'why' to something. I was conducting a diversity and inclusion session and a guy had an 'ah ha' moment. There are many definitions of 'ah ha' moments. Oprah Winfrey tagged that saying and states that it is a moment of sudden realization, inspiration, insight, recognition, or comprehension of something that you already knew. That is the most important part, you already know it, but it may be buried or hidden. So, this guy had an 'ah ha' moment. During class he disclosed that he didn't give a person who was overweight a promotion. I was shocked to hear it. It slipped out before he had a chance to pull it back in. So, he spent the next few minutes explaining why. He went on to say that people who were heavy set showed a lack of concern for themselves, so they couldn't possibly care about their job. There was more said, but it all added up to a little fuzzy thinking and prejudice. He came to me during the break and disclosed that he was obese as a young man until he decided to go into the military and lost all his weight and became a gym rat. He now sees people who are overweight as fat and lazy. The 'ah ha' moment was when he discovered that he really had a fear of becoming overweight again. This took some digging but that was where we ended up after a lengthy discussion. This self-awareness is that he doesn't like 'fat' people. Self-understanding was not about them but about him. Self-knowledge was that he was afraid of becoming that which he despised, and he despised it because deep down he still saw himself as that. Now, the final piece is self-acceptance. He must accept that he was hard on people who were overweight because of his own insecurities. Once he could accept his truth then he could change.

Change cannot occur without these three factors in play. He must accept it to change it. But, if he doesn't accept that insight as a truth then he cannot change what doesn't exist, right? This means he cannot and will not manage his biases about heavy people. We can pretty much figure out that nothing good will come of this in the long-term. Thankfully that 'ah ha' moment exposed the three areas, and he was willing to change, especially since he discovered that this was less about them and more about him.

There may be several reoccurring situations that prevent you from moving forward or even playing the game that has nothing to do with the game, but rather your outlook on the game or what someone is requiring of you. To step back and examine what you feel, think, believe, etc. is a start. Then face up to the reality of why you feel, think, believe, etc. to understand why. You need to dig deep to know where your reaction/response to something is coming from and then own up to it. Some people don't like the game because it feels too much like being controlled, and if you have control issues and pride yourself on rebellion then yeah, you are going to have a challenging time embracing the game (smile).

The point is, how can you make an intelligent choice when you lack self-management? You will be tossed and turned while encountering the game and true players. Spend a little time understanding what makes you tick and what ticks you off, and more importantly, why. I mentioned in an earlier book that you should know what makes your boss tick and what ticks her off, but it is more important to know that of yourself.

The previous two books were more external while this book is more internal. It's less about being controlled, influenced or manipulated, but rather taking control. And that, my friend, is all about the choices you make.

For absolute clarity, let me say this again, I do not advocate the game and I don't particularly like having to be the messenger of the game, either. I do enjoy helping people succeed, so the message resonates with me. I've learned along the way that I will encounter gate keepers as I continue pursuing my career goals and objectives. Those gate keepers can be an employer, a client, someone with influence, someone with authority, etc. You are never in a positon where someone doesn't have some say in what you can and cannot do, if there is monetary gain attached. Even though I own a company, I have to meet certain expectations and requirements.

Recently, I was invited to speak at a MNC law firm, in Singapore. The woman who invited me to speak on Playing by the Unwritten Rules was a gate keeper, so it was important to appease her in an effort to develop a vendor relationship. After my presentation, I received overwhelmingly positive responses from attendees. As a follow-up, I was speaking to the woman who invited me to present. She kept saying that everyone said the session was fun and that I was humorous, but I could tell there was something else going on. She added that she had gotten negative feedback and that I set them back regarding unconscious bias based on my tattoo reference. I asked her if those people who commented negatively truly heard what I said. I went on to say that bias is the whole point. Unwritten rules are often bias, as are other things that aren't always fair and so forth, but they are a reality. I'm very transparent in keeping it real for audiences. What I shared with them is that my old company's policy based on my preference, was to not hire professionals in leadership positions who had visible tattoos. My client base in the US was very conservative. You would not see a CNN reporter with a tattoo peeking out from her blouse or a general working at the Pentagon giving a briefing with a tattoo wrapped around his wrist. It ain't gonna happen. Maybe one day, we will see high ranking officials and high-level professionals with tattoos; but for now, I have to play the game with the clients I have selected to serve and align with. The woman went on to give an example of how the complainer said that there are plenty of people in their company who have tattoos. Well, what that means is that that rule in particular doesn't apply to her organization, but it doesn't change that it applies to the Pentagon, military executives, CNN reporters, etc. Rules are fluid depending on your organization, and I used my company as a reference, not as a standard. In fact, I want one for myself. I have the perfect image, but I haven't figured out exactly where I want it, right? I still have to strike a balance between what I want and what my clients expect. Now, to some this may seem hypocritical, if you heard me speak about my hiring practices. I will not hire anyone for a leadership role with a visible tattoo, right? And, this was not in my employee handbook, but it was understood by all decision-makers in my company. So, I must reiterate the reason why I was unable to hire a leader with a visible tattoo was because they would have to engage an ultra-conservative clientele which helped me to keep the lights on and employees employed. I have worked with NASA, CIA, FAA, Army, Homeland Security, Pentagon, etc. These are clients who take image very seriously and equate image to credibility. How credible would I or my employee look giving a presentation with a nose ring and I love my mom written across our necks? To some that would be fine, but I know my clients who are not millennials, but rather they are traditionalists and baby boomers who are conservative. They need to believe and trust that when I hold a contract that exceeds a million dollars, I will make sound decisions.

Unfortunately, people have biases and judgments that have nothing to do with your ability to perform. If decision-makers are busy having a conversation in their head about your hair, tattoos, piercing, weight, or any number of things that may impact them personally, they aren't going to hear what you are saying. You are getting in the way of yourself. As much as I like tasteful body art, it's not encouraged in my line of work. So, I gently pushed back with this woman, who then became short with me. I wrote her an email apologizing if I had insulted her. I stated that maybe her company is not a good fit, but the rules are designed to cause people to have conversations and to look at their organizations. I said all that to say this: that's the whole thing about the unwritten rules. There are rules within whatever environment or industry you choose to align. So, understand yourself and equally understand where you opt to be employed. Even though tattoos maybe fine within this company, I assure you that there are some preferences practiced that may be imposed on others that may seem quite reasonable but are actually unreasonable. The net-net of this story: she wrote back and acknowledged that her behavior was rude and that in fact it wasn't people; it was one guy who had issues.

Well, if you understand the bell curve theory, you'll understand that not everyone will agree with everything. Actually, 15% of a group will find what I'm saying to be hog wash and 15% will find what I am saying as the most provocative thing they have ever heard, and then the rest in the middle will have various opinions. For the most part, people usually get it. Although, I try to spend time getting people to understand and to listen without filters. To do this I even wrap it around jokes and humor. I find a spoon full of sugar helps the medicine to go down. In short, the message is that if you have control over how you show up then make a decision on whether certain battles, positions and/or stands are worth the fight. Sometimes the juice isn't worth the squeeze or the squeeze isn't worth the juice. I learned that earlier on in my career. Some things aren't as important as achieving my ultimate goal which is to build a thriving practice, work on projects that I love and retire with wealth to write about subjects that I'm passionate about. I can't get there if I can't earn an above average income because I didn't want to play the game. You can't always do what you want to get what you want, is all I'm saying.

> **Exercise:**
>
> **Take a moment to write down the many things you want to accomplish in your career and in life. Now, brainstorm all that will be expected of you, such as volunteering for assignments, relocating, presenting to groups, etc. and then write down what you will need to do to change or achieve it, e.g. take classes on presenting, working later than usual, attending functions and networking, etc.**

I wanted to work internationally; that opportunity presented itself, not necessarily by choice. That meant relocating and launching a business in Asia to be totally immersed. What was expected of me? It was expected that I would understand the Asian culture. Now that's pretty broad. There are many cultures here; diversity is vast. I was told that I was expected to have less American stories and more stories applicable to Asia. There are several changes afoot. First, I needed to change from an American-centric focus to a more glocal (global/local) focus. We aren't the center of the Earth, nor do we hold the cherished title of economic powerhouse any longer. I needed to embrace where I live and learn the customs, traditions and culture. It isn't easy, but it is necessary because I chose to be here. Secondly, the change I had to make was to appear less conservative in dress. What actually worked in the US was off putting here.

I'm in a Muslim country so women don't wear Brook Brothers suits. I used to wear ascots, tailored suits in pinstripe fabric, etc. and cuff links for God's sake. I wanted to look as gender neutral as possible to fit in at the table, but I don't need the Western hard corporate look anymore. I need to look feminine. While on a panel at a large conference in Singapore, I shared with an audience of women that as I grew my company in the US, I had to look like my clients who were men. A man on the panel with me stated that women do not have to look like men to succeed. He was right to some extent, but he didn't know my story. I needed to look gender neutral because I was horribly sexually harassed when I was younger, and I looked like a kid when I started my business back in 1995. If I begin writing about the sexual harassment that I experienced in the US Marine Corps and as a business owner working in a male dominated environment, I would have another book.

Trust me, back then I needed to change my look! When I was younger, the style was mid-length skirts. I rocked a skirt like Tina Turner. I was sexy, but sexy didn't work for me. I had to evaluate what the men thought they were buying or rather what I was selling. So, I became conservative to avoid the verbal abuse, sexual innuendos, and yes, inappropriate touching. Yes, it happened! Women are sexually harassed. When I covered up by wearing suits, shirts with an ascot or scarf, that sent a different message. In my opinion, I was practicing situational judgment. Now that I'm over 50, I don't receive that same type of treatment. Yet, I'm still always mindful of how I'm showing up; my presence and my brand matter.

You'll hear this story again. I call it the pink versus purple shirt story: kinda like the red pill or the blue pill in *The Matrix*. Well, not really. But, it's a good story. Recently, I was getting dressed for a meeting with a shipping company out of Europe. The meeting room would be filled with men except one woman from

HR, and I recalled the VP of HR, a man, asking me whether I can identify and relate to men since it will be mostly men on the vessels. I was able to talk about my military experience and clientele that were male dominated. The fact that the question was asked showed that there were still some prejudgments about a woman working with men out at sea. While getting dressed the morning of the presentation, I had an option of wearing a pink or a purple shirt. Both shirts would be accented with a scarf, but one sent the message of soft while the other was a little stronger. This isn't Dr. Indigo talking; this is psychology. Wearing a pink shirt into that boardroom would not have served me well. So, when someone says a woman doesn't have to look like a man; that's right. Unfortunately, in the world that I live in at this day and time, I can't always look like a girl. Sometimes, I must be neutral. No one can tell you or me what is right or wrong when it comes to playing the game for ourselves. It's neither right nor wrong, but rather our choices. We must make choices based on the space we are in, who is/are players in the game and what are we trying to achieve. Choices.

I made the choice to wear the purple shirt. It didn't hurt, and it didn't kill me. Did I want to wear the pink shirt? Truthfully, yes. I had already worn the purple shirt on that trip, and the pink shirt was fresh. And, I can rock the color pink like no other. However, the pink could have caused questions in the minds of those men in attendance who already believe women cannot handle a room full of men. I attempted to take away any excuses or biases they could unconsciously and/or consciously have about women on ships. I can't change hearts and minds, but I can minimize distractions; it's merely situational judgement. As I told this story, which is a part of my signature presentation, I literally had a woman walk out after disagreeing vehemently that she would have worn the pink shirt. Before storming out, she went on to say how she wouldn't want a client that had biases. At that point, I knew to stop trying to get her on board and to let her abandon ship. However, at another event, during the break, a woman empathized with me regarding this story. She said, "It's not as if you didn't own the shirt. You obviously wear pink because you packed it. So, you were being yourself despite what others may think. You just had options and you chose what you wanted for that occasion." Situational judgement is all I can write to this point.

People make this game thing far more complicated than it has to be. You don't have a choice about playing the game, but you do have a choice on how you will play. The game exists with or without you. The game was there before you got there and will be there when you are gone. However, through success and power, you can change the game. Yet, it will still be a game, right? It then becomes a game; wherein, you are making the rules.

Chapter 1: The Difficulty in Life is the Choices

I hope one day the unwritten rules are obsolete because everyone will be judged by the merit of their character, there will be no biases, and people will be given equal opportunity to show their worth, and be valued and respected by such. But, that's not the world in which we live. There are biases, there are people who want to be first or best, and there is a game. Now the choice is, how are you going to play the game?

Before we go any further, let me introduce the concept of journaling. Whenever I speak to women audiences or coach individuals, I recommend that people journal. I have journaled for years, and I actually have taught my sons to journal. I believe that true journaling allows you to be authentic, transparent and honest to a fault. When you put pen to paper, not typing, but actually writing, you open yourself and your mind to a different space. You give yourself permission to be more honest with the journal than with yourself. You seem to write with truth and recall based on what is your reality, versus trying to remember stuff down the road, which changes over time. Journals capture what is going on at the time, like a picture. Let's be honest. People do lie, and some people even lie to themselves. It seems creepy to lie in a journal because you are talking to yourself. As Mark Twain said, "If you tell the truth, you don't have to remember anything." If you lie to yourself while recording your history, then please don't waste your time with this book. I'm providing guidance for you to be a better person and professional, and if lying is a part of your game, then what I have to share will run counter to what and who you are.

I tell people to purchase a journal that speaks to them. What I mean is select something that makes you feel good. Maybe it's the color, thickness, print or whatever. You need something that you like picking up and holding so that you welcome going to it regularly. I write in two distinct journals. One journal is to capture my thoughts and feelings on a regular basis. I never recommend to anyone to write in their journal with a set schedule, etc. That becomes a daunting chore when you don't feel like you have anything to write. Just commit to visiting your journal frequently or on a regular base, which is subjective, right?

I can see where I have written every day for months. Then, I may not have written for months because life took over and I lost track of time. But, I have two journals, right? That is what works for me. In one journal, I usually write/talk about my life and my career. As a side note, my life and career were one for a very long time. Now, my career and life are distinguishable. In short, I now have a life separate from work (smile). Then I have a second style of writing within the other journal. I write to my great great grandchildren. Get this: I don't have any grandchildren at this point, but when or if I do, I want them to know who I am. I write as if they are getting my journal as a piece of history. Think about it. Wouldn't you love to read about your great great-grandparent in their own words, and not what others have written about their generation, race, group, etc.?

I often wonder what life was really like for my great great grandmother. She was an African-American woman from the Deep South who was probably a slave, but her children were born as free men or women after the civil war. That's pretty much all I know, and even that is speculation. There's nothing factual demonstrating that the people I have come to know as my family are even my biological kin because my great grandmother could have been adopted. Okay, I'm going off on a tangent. You get the point. I know nothing for certain about my heritage, people or family. But, if I could read what she was thinking and how she felt that could help me understand myself, the world and so much more than what I know. So, I share with my great great grandchildren who I am. My journal details how I became a success, how I fell and failed, how I loved and lost, how I loved and won, and my career as a black woman from America, now in Asia. It speaks of how I launched a company and found myself through trials and tribulations to help others to freedom. So, yeah, I write to the future.

For instance, I spoke at Google about my career journey. I love Google! I call myself a Googler. Although, when I spoke at Google, I learned that their employees are called Googlers. I guess I made myself an honorary Googler. The point is…when I spoke at Google, I mentioned it in my journal because I was so excited and honored. When I wrote about my experience at Google on its stage, I had to first discuss what is a Google and what is Google because both may morph into something else in 100+ years or not even exist, and people won't know what I'm talking about. When I write I explain things to help the future reader understand the times in which I am living and how I live during this time in history. It is therapeutic because I am so honest and open.

I want you to select a style of writing and then journal. It doesn't have to be a future style of writing, but rather an opportunity to occasionally capture some thoughts, feelings and beliefs. It is so cleansing to journal because it is introspective. You will say things in your journal that you wouldn't even tell a therapist. Now, here's the warning! Don't let people at your job know about your journal. A journal can be used as evidence in a court case/law suit. The courts recognized that you are documenting information that could help prove or disprove a case. So, your journal may be submitted as evidence. Yikes! Keep your journal confidential and locked up is what I would recommend. No one needs that kind of access into your head. There's a saying that you cannot beat an enemy who has an outpost in your head. I was happily married until it wasn't so happy any more. Don't let anyone have an open invitation to your most inner thoughts, fears, joy, etc. because it could be used against you. Basically, in any conflict that has cost me dearly…I lost because the other person knew my thoughts, fears and weaknesses and leveraged them against me. This is what I think: people are for the most part genuinely good. This is what I know: when they can see an opportunity to take what you have or become jealous, the game shifts and they can do things that may hurt you.

A journal should be taken seriously and treated with an elevated level of respect. Every page you write is worth it. Nothing is more rewarding than going through your journal to see how far you have come and the choices you have made along the way. I am spending time discussing the importance of a journal because it allows you to see what circumstances were presented, the choices you made and the consequences of your decisions over an extended period of time.

Exercise:

I encourage you to go to a book store and purchase a journal to accompany this book. As you continue to read this book, write about what you are learning, feeling and experiencing. I want you to write a few pages about your career journey. Start with the most relevant turn in your career and jot down some memorable points that got you from there to here. Then as you read through this book, jot down some ideas on what you can do differently to improve your career and life based on some of my discussions. That will help you to get into the habit of writing. As my son Sinclair would say, "Write through all of your emotions and not just the good or the bad."

Remember, that everything is about choices as you read through this book, as you accomplish the day-to-day activities of your job, and especially through the changes you will make as a result of reading this book.

Chapter 2

Uncommon Unwritten Rules

I continue to enjoy a wonderful career and I attribute much of my success to my ability to play the game and to my passion for bringing awareness to the game. I started a company called Careers In Transition, Inc. in 1995. I grew it from a home-based business to a thriving multi-million dollar enterprise with contracts ranging from 1.5 million to 18 million dollars. The foundation of my company was based on helping people transition from one company to another when US companies were downsizing in the 1990s. That grew into providing products and services that helped organizations attract, develop and retain talent. As I worked closely with decision-makers and leaders, they consistently had the same issues and concerns with their employees. I was able to sum it up as their employees simply not understanding the game.

Initially, I wrote my first book merely as a way of giving my clients some insight into reoccurring problems they were having with their employees. I sat down and started to write some thoughts which eventually turned into a book. I realized that I couldn't give that away, so I finished the writings and began the process of getting the book published. I boast of one client buying 1,000 books of each title, which then led to a multi-million dollar change management initiative built around the book series. I remember at a conference, a young professional purchased my book and came back in the next two days and said, "I finished the book. What else do you have that I can read? I learned so much." So, I wrote the second book which still left people wanting more. That led to keynote presentations and signature talks. It has been an exciting experience of changing lives through my books. I can go on and on about the positive things I've heard, but that's not why you are reading this book. But I wanted to set the tone. The book series has been incredibly successful, and I'm excited about writing this last edition to the three-part series, which spans a couple of decades which is what I'm trying to convey.

As one of my favorite comedians, Joan Rivers, would ask, "Can we talk?" For the most part, people join an organization in hopes of having a thriving career. Now there are some who go into a company to get their ticket stamped for the next gig or with other ulterior motives. There are only a few people who go through the entire hiring process to be a failure, to sabotage, to draw unemployment or execute whatever crazy scheme they have up their sleeves, but by and large, people join an organization in hopes of being a success. So, what happens between signing all the HR docs and getting your employee handbook when you start the job to signing all the HR docs to get your last check when you no longer work for the company?

No one tells employees how to play the game by the unwritten rules. It's not about your age, position or any variety of diversity aspects. It's about being new to that culture and recognizing the game that is being played. Unfortunately, successful professionals often don't see themselves as playing the game or requiring people to play the game, so they don't or rather won't coach from that perspective. As I say in all of my signature presentations on the unwritten rules, companies have an employee handbook to give you the written rules which helps you to keep a job, while the unwritten rules help you to be promotable. If an employee doesn't see progression, it will be a matter of time before she leaves or even sabotages; sad but true. I started coaching leaders about the game, and it eventually became a platform and passion for me.

I feel as if I must give a disclaimer. I neither like nor support the game or unwritten rules. I will repeat this again, as a gentle reminder that this is merely a reality and not something that I condone. Because it is real, it would be a shame for me to know how to help people achieve measurable success but withhold the information because it is something that people are uncomfortable hearing and addressing. Playing the game has made me a very wealthy woman, so I know that it works. It has become the foundation for many of my projects, but it has been met with criticism and skepticism from people who either have not achieved success because they don't want to play, or people who simply don't understand it. Oddly enough, I've never met anyone who is successful that denies playing the game and/or playing by the unwritten rules to some extent. I've had people state that they don't do this or that, but when I start describing certain behaviors or actions, they will sometimes cautiously admit that they do those things to get ahead; thus, they play the game.

Let me reemphasize: the game itself is not good or bad. It's the people within the game who cause distress, distrust, etc. So, don't hate the game: hate the player. I don't make up the game or the rules…I merely know how to play the game by the unwritten rules and I do what I need to do, to do what I want to do. It really is about choices of whether you will, or you won't play by the unwritten rules, but don't get it twisted…you are playing the game. As I keep saying, you are playing the game as soon as you show up for work and it is a full court press. You are not excused from the game based on your age, ethnicity, gender, race, position or title. And, the game changes with every level within every organization. The game has numerous connotations and expectations based on the previous diversity aspects.

I have seen people who have crashed and burned in the game while others continue to win at the game. There will be some winners and takers in this thing called 'the game'. Sometimes you'll be on top and sometimes you're going to get knocked down. Ultimately, it's about getting up and playing your game with integrity, authenticity and even compassion, at least for me. As I shared in the last book, the rules are unwritten for a myriad of reasons ranging from simple preference to being illegal. This is where you may want to go back and read the second book which lists all the reasons and explanations on why rules are unwritten. You always have a choice on how you will play the game and basically, where you will play the game. If something is unethical, there is nothing written or unwritten that says you must remain in that situation. You always have options. You'll hear this again throughout this book; you have three choices when confronted with things that make you uncomfortable because they are either unethical, biased, illegal, and so forth: 1.) You can stay and take it; 2.) Stay and change it, or 3.) Leave. Trust me, there are consequences to each of these choices, yet the choice is yours.

When you figure out the game that is being played, which is merely the culture, then you can determine how you are going to play, based on who you are as a professional and as a person. People get swept away and lost in the game because they don't know who they truly are and lack the courage to be authentic coupled with situational judgment. I've made some choices that weren't in my best interests, but it was the game and I wanted in. There were also times when I walked away because I was unwilling to play by a set of rules that ran counter to my beliefs or needs. What I can say is that each move and decision was based on my understanding of me and what I wanted out of my career. There were prizes and trophies for some of the wins I gained and heavy losses for some things that I did or chose not to do. As one quote I read said, "I don't regret the things I did wrong. I regret the good things I did for the wrong people." I'll explain why that is relevant, in a later chapter. At any rate, whatever the trophy you are in pursuit of acquiring, just know that once you get it, you need to be okay with what you went through to get it. I have found following your true north will keep you on the right path.

As I mentioned in the Introduction, this is the final book in this series. I simply want to share my journey and discuss the things that I've learnt along the way because it may be of benefit to you in some way. Again, I want to put a little context around some things from the first two books. I'm always asked what exactly are the unwritten rules. There are no hard and fast unwritten rules. The rules are based on your industry, your organization, your company, your boss, etc. You can have great success in one part of an organization, get promoted to another department, and then find yourself failing miserably not because of competence but rather the game switched up on you based on your new seat assignment and new players with their own unwritten rules. Don't fret. I can share with you some baseline rules that have been shared over the years during my participative workshops/keynotes.

Often, during my sessions, I have the audience break off into small groups and they are challenged to come up with unwritten rules that they know of in their organization or in general. Some interesting things emerge during that exercise. However, sometimes people give an unwritten rule that is either a gripe or simply incorrect. For instance, just a month ago a seasoned professional said, "It is okay to embarrass your boss when something needs to be said." I asked her to explain. She gave a very good reason for why something should be said when others are silent. However, I can't agree with embarrassing your boss. An unwritten rule across all industries is to never embarrass your boss. Keep in mind that the higher your boss is, the more ego she may have, so embarrassing her will not serve you well. Think about it. Do you like to be embarrassed? In fact, would you admit that once you become embarrassed you listen less to what the person is saying because you become more concerned with how people may be perceiving you at that moment?

There are tactful and diplomatic ways to deal with sensitive topics, situations and matters in general, yeah? I shared with the participant that you can't get to heaven by dragging people through hell. You don't have to hurt, embarrass or embellish to be effectively heard. She then gave another example on why she would embarrass her boss. She went on to explain that her intent is not to embarrass her boss, but there may be something that he needs to know, which may embarrass him when pointed out. Really? I thought to myself, did you not hear what I just said? We can unintentionally embarrass someone which can be met with the same outcome of intentionally embarrassing someone. Here's what I suggest: if you are in a meeting and what is being said is inaccurate or causing the boss to look uninformed, you can do several things. In an assertive non-aggressive manner, say to the person speaking, "Excuse me. May we take a break? I would like to share with you some information offline/in private that may be of benefit to this discussion." Or, you can write down your concern, fold up the paper and pass it to him. Trust me, he will read your secret note. And, you can use nonverbal cues to request him to chat offline outside the meeting room. Then there is the direct-indirect approach. You can say, "Excuse me, Mike. You stated XYZ. Now, I'm just thinking aloud. Have you considered ABC, based on LMNOP?" Depending on what comes next you should know whether to shut it down or speak up. Saying that you are thinking aloud sends the message that you weren't hiding in the bushes to lunge into a full-frontal attack, and it gives your boss a chance to save face by your not being married to your idea or information. There are numerous ways to share information that you believe is relevant and important, but embarrassment should not be your go-to stance. Believe me when I say that you will get your ass handed to you; maybe not in that instance, but at some point, that embarrassment will come back to haunt you. Hmm… maybe that was a bit harsh. But, I've seen careers go down in flames or die a slow death because someone was embarrassed, and she had to flex her muscles to make sure it won't happen again.

Let me give you an example of an unwritten rule that was a part of the game that speaks to inclusion, which I wrote about in the second book but want to reiterate with a different story. I was on a panel at the Women's Forum Singapore, just last week. I met the Executive President of the Women's Forum for the Economy and Society. We were sitting talking about everything from being working moms to being corporate successes. This woman is a very successful businesswoman from France whom I admire and who was working in America at some point in her career. She shared with me a time when she was standing amongst a group of men who were talking about stuff, in general and nothing of significance. One guy was telling a story and all the guys laughed. Now, keep in mind that she was the only woman and she was not an American. She didn't understand certain references to a television show that the men found funny. So, she asked the guy next to her what was funny. He was polite enough and wanting to be inclusive, he explained what was funny. Then the guy talking said something else and again everyone laughed and again she needed an explanation which the guy again had no problem giving. Then soon after one laughter another laughter followed. This time, she just laughed. Now, that is playing the game. She wanted to be included and they wanted to be inclusive. You have to meet people half way, which is the noblest distance to travel. She could have kept asking for an explanation, which would have shown that she was not truly a part of the group, based on her limited cultural understanding, or she could have killed the vibe. That wouldn't have served her. What I admire is that (1) she stayed and didn't slink off to her office, (2) she didn't try to change the subject to suit her needs and, (3) she understood the importance of being one of the guys. I am most assured that she has had profound international success based on her ability to be a chameleon when required. There are many thought-provoking points to her story. But, what I want you to understand is that it didn't change who she was, nor was it an affront to her character. She played the damn game, which is what I'm trying to get so many people who are socially, economically or ethnically disadvantaged to understand and appreciate. Sometimes we hold on to our pride so hard that our career cracks from the pressure. Seriously, it's just a game and it's not that serious! You can make it hard for yourself or easy. I choose to "let it be easy" which I'll write about a little more in the Indigoism chapter.

Unwritten rules are unwritten for a myriad of reasons as outlined in the second book. Often, they are unbeknownst to people. So, don't be shocked that some of the following rules may be entirely foreign to you. Again, you may have an employee handbook that discusses written rules. There may even be a paragraph or two that talks about the promotion process, but it will not tell you to support your boss so that you are an invaluable resource to her and the organization. That is an unwritten rule that everyone who is politically savvy knows, professionals who are in the know know, and decision-makers think that you know. Now keep in mind that there is absolutely nothing for certain in this matter. It's very subjective and fluid. What I say may resonate with one person and totally upset another. So, embrace what makes sense and just be mindful of what doesn't pertain to you or rather doesn't serve as a general truth for you. Use your own judgment and understanding based on YOU! If you recall, I said in the previous book that YOU means 'Years of Understanding'. If you find yourself annoyed or uncomfortable with something, highlight it and drill deeper to figure out what is it about that rule that creates an emotion. You may find that you have either broken that rule, don't believe that it is fair, or you are not in a company or industry where it is relevant. This is worth giving pause in order to understand it more. Keep in mind that unwritten rules are rules that are *not written* and sometimes not even discussed; however, people assume that you know. So, without further ado, here are some classic unwritten rules that I have heard, seen or practiced over the years, mixed with a few uncommon unwritten rules:

1. **Constantly Develop and Manage Your Career**

    Career management and career development are not one and the same. You develop your career to manage your career. You increase your bench strength to make appropriate planned out strategic moves, which is managing your career. It is not the responsibility of the organization to do this for you; it is the company's responsibility to afford you the opportunity and resources to develop. Sometimes, to really get what you want, you may need to pay out-of-pocket and make an investment in yourself. It's your career; not the organization's career. You can't complain that you aren't ready for the next level because the company will not send you to a particular class, etc. That is what you want and need. The company may be fine with you being in the job that you are in, so you must invest in yourself to earn that next promotion or sustainable success. Also, don't ever ever abdicate responsibility for your career progression. It is your career and no one, I repeat, no one will care as much as you or know what you need when you need it.

2. **Don't Perpetuate Stereotypes**

    During a session, a group of women engineers said that an unwritten rule is to never bring baked goodies to meetings, offer to take notes or do anything that has the stereotype associated with being a woman. They went on to say that once you do it then the men expect that from you and stop treating you as an equal significant contributor, but more like their mom, wife, or any role that traditionally serves men. 'Don't bring the baked goods if you are a woman in a male-dominated environment' is a rule. This further reinforces the stereotypes placed on women that they have fought years to overcome. If you are in a management/leadership meeting where you are among a few women and the request for a note taker is thrown out there; don't you be the one to raise your hand to take the notes. You are not a clerical, administrative professional. I'm not saying that there is anything wrong with being an administrative professional, but people in general treat admin staff differently from physicians, engineers, executives, etc. When you raise that pen you lower your clout and positional power within that circle. Women who are in STEM (Science, Technology, Engineering and Mathematics) often have to demonstrate their abilities time and time again; to bring in the baked goods sends a subliminal message of being Suzy Homemaker. Keep in mind some men, albeit cavemen, still believe women should not be in certain male-dominated environments and the last remaining Neanderthals think women should be at home with the children. So, don't feed into any potential biased views by playing a role that they assign to women who are not considered career-minded polished professionals, in their view. That is not your role.

This is the perfect time to add that when I make such references, it does not mean I am of a particular opinion, but rather I'm giving you insight into how some people think. So, read without blinders or filters to hear what I am saying. In fact, I wrote how I wanted to bring a watermelon to a picnic when I was married to a Marine Corps officer who was tasked with bringing the dessert. He was mortified that we would walk into the picnic with a watermelon, further deepening the stereotype ascribed to Black people. So, we took a nice, unbiased pie, right? As small and insignificant as this may sound to someone who is not Black, keep in mind that rules have various implications for different people. Women have stereotypes that they must overcome in the game, too. In fact, diversity continues to a play a role in what games are played and how they are played based on several diversity dimensions such as age, race, gender, ethnicity, education, marital status, etc.

3. **Shop Your Idea Before the Meeting**

    If you find that your projects or ideas aren't getting support, it may be that you aren't getting buy-in behind the scenes before taking it to the masses. Sometimes you need to take your idea to several people before the meeting and pitch and solicit their support. Some people have votes sewn up before they present their ideas and you are wondering why their message got pushed forward and your message is lying on the table needing resuscitation. Your colleague, who may by and large be your competition, pitched his idea and asked for support and even made changes that would prevent push back before he took it into the meeting. You went in naively thinking all was above board and you got push back without time to make corrections, so a decision was made based on what was wrapped up with a bow and ready to go. This is the real world. Don't be fooled; your contemporaries are your competition. Think about a professional sports team. The goal is for the players to win the game as a team, but they compete against each other to get more playing time, etc. It's just a part of the game. It's not personal. What you propose may be exceptional, but you want to garner support to make sure you are not blindsided or upstaged.

4. **Choose Your Seat Carefully at the Meeting**

   I have mentioned the power seat in the last book, but this is slightly different. When I'm on a sales call or someone is coming into my office to pitch, I arrange my team strategically. One person is in front of the decision-maker to read her nonverbals while close enough to me so that he can tap my leg or foot to get my attention. I hate to admit that there is the table top game that everyone sees in the room, and then there is the game that no one sees under the table that uses nonverbals, etc. This requires sitting in strategic places during the meeting. What you are trying to accomplish will determine who sits where. But, what is most important is to have a seat at the table literally and figuratively. I've seen where a boardroom can only accommodate up to a certain number of people at the table and then there are chairs against the wall around the room. Don't sit in those chairs for heaven's sake. Be at the table where you will be seen and even heard. Making sure you have a seat at the table is a part of your job if you want to truly play the game. It's being seen. It's not who you know but who knows you. If you find that those seats are taken, get to meetings early!

5. **Let Others Hear What You are Thinking**

   If you are presenting, make sure you have a place at the table that is strategic. Being in the room and sitting at the table aren't enough. You have to show up by sharing your thoughts. This is particularly tough for introverts. Some people are not presenting their own ideas; someone else is presenting for them. That is the worst mistake you can make as a professional. Think about a time when you were placed on a group project and no one wanted to present. So, the extrovert said that he would represent the group. He presented the final project and whether he was a true contributor or not he received the accolades. There is value placed on who tells the tale. Be at the table and speak up. I tell groups that there are the 4-Ss to communicate directly with strength: Stand up, Speak up, Shut up and Sit down. This quick formula will take you far whether you are an introvert or extrovert. It allows you to speak up without rambling which happens when you are not comfortable addressing an audience. The second point is for introverts while the third point is for extroverts. One doesn't say enough while the other sometimes says too much.

6. **Don't Gossip**

   The grape vine exists in all organizations and it is a legitimate platform for communicating. Interestingly, I suggest that you stay and listen to the gossip if it is not too negative and/or about your boss. You do not want to be seen in a group that is undermining your boss or the company. Yet, you do want to be perceived as one of the boys/girls. You will learn a lot of things by hearing about what is going on in a company, etc., but gossip is referred to as the grape vine. Similar to a grape vine found in nature, you can pick from the vine, but you cannot add grapes to the vine. In short, do not add to the gossip. Also, don't stay too long; just long enough to capture some juicy information that can help you understand what is happening in the organization and show that you are a part of the team. This is where professionals make mistakes and don't mingle around the water cooler or wherever people gather in an organization. People need to see that you are seeing yourself as a part of the team, even if you don't say anything while in their presence. If they ask you for your opinion or to divulge what you know, just state that you are not clear on what they are asking, you are not at liberty to say or that you aren't comfortable speaking about it. But, whatever you do, don't lie by saying that you don't know something when you do. That can come back to haunt you.

7. **Mingle Not Huddle**

In professional sports, players come together to strategize while on the field. This is called getting in a huddle. The point is that they are team members planning how to play against the opposing team. Unfortunately, I have seen people huddle in the workplace. I hear that huddling has become the catch phrase, which makes sense when the huddle is to work as a team. But, when people huddle with the intent to exclude others or create little cliques, that will, in time, cost you. Teammates huddle, right? However, if you exclude someone who is on your team, huddling takes on a negative connotation. So, to be clear, make sure you are mingling with others when a gathering doesn't have to be solely for team members. That means talking with various people, dropping by several people's desks through the day and asking people to join in on conversations when you and a few people are standing in a general area. If you want to be a master game player, you need to mingle and not just huddle (period).

Now, tie that in with gossip. If there are negative things being said, then excuse yourself and let them know that something is pending on your desk. When they are talking about things in general, just listen for a while before going back to your desk or wherever you need to be. I once worked in a place, where, at 4 pm without fail everyone came out of their office or cubicle to sit in this particular area to talk. They were really sitting there to count down to the time to leave, in my opinion. But, they were mingling because everyone was expected to be there, and all were included. In a huddle, only a few are allowed into that circle. They looked forward to mingling so that they could catch up, laugh and chat about matters in general. I saw it as a total waste of time because I had work to do. Someone pulled my coattail to say that people saw me as disconnected, as if I thought I was too good to sit with them and that I was making them look bad because they weren't working. So, I would stop what I was doing and sit there and chat for a moment, and then I gave a reason to go somewhere else when I felt that I had been there long enough to appease them. Now, you may be wondering why I would do that. Sometimes your peers can become your boss, sometimes peers are able to suggest people for projects, and sometimes bosses want to see if you can play in the sandbox with others. It was my boss who shared with me how the others perceived my not hanging out with them. It was merely an unwritten rule that employees would hang out in the communal area at the end of the workday for that department within that organization, and it didn't cause me distress to do it.

8. An Open-Door Policy Doesn't Necessarily Mean Open to You

Managers and leaders will allow people to feel free to come in to see them. However, you may have a boss who is not comfortable with you going around him. If you want to talk to his boss, let him know. Say something to the effect of, "Cheryl said that we could drop by her office to discuss matters with her. Would you mind if I pay her a visit?" Your boss is going to ask you why. Just be honest because whatever you are going to say is going to get back to your boss anyway. You would rather your information come from you than his boss. But, in my opinion, I would go to my boss to have a conversation, first. The only time I would go to my boss's boss is when something isn't getting resolved, and I have one foot out the door at this point. I hope this makes sense.

9. Don't Exclude People

We aren't in high school. Don't make people feel overlooked and unimportant. If you don't like that person, just limit your time with her. Don't make it a point to invite the person sitting to her right and the person sitting to her left out for lunch while she just sits there watching you leave with colleagues. Extend an invite, hope she doesn't come, but offer. At some point, that person may oversee a project that you want in on or worst, she becomes your boss. As Maya Angelou stated, "I've learned that people will forget what you said, people will forget what you did, but people will never forget how you made them feel." Can you recall a time when you were excluded? I'm sure it didn't feel good. I would make it a point to drop by everyone's desk and even ask various people to walk with me to get coffee. No one is asking you to have an arranged marriage between your son and that person's daughter. It's not that serious. It would behoove you to practice inclusion with everyone. Gestures of exclusion can be as minor as telling a joke that you have told to nearly everyone in the office, but you skip over the colleague who is eavesdropping by saying, "You won't find this funny." Tell him the joke, too. Be consistent and be inclusive.

10. Don't Choose a Side: Be Switzerland

As I shared in the first book, you should never witness your boss having an argument with a colleague, because you may not know their true relationship. What may seem like a heated argument between a peer and your boss may actually be a lovers' spat. You could hear something that they didn't intend for you to hear, and now they have to get rid of the evidence, i.e. you. It may not be this deep, but regardless of who it is, be diplomatic and don't choose a side, even if they try to corner you into pledging your allegiance to one of them. At best, maybe share the benefits of both sides but express your confidence that they'll come to the right decision based on hearing each other out and then excuse yourself. This is really about being in a no-win situation. You cannot win anything from choosing a side; someone will inevitably resent your decision or at a minimum maybe feel slighted.

11. Have a Mentor and an Advocate, Separately

A mentor shares with you information to help you improve performance and increase productivity, as well as strategize. An advocate opens doors for you and speaks on your behalf in your absence. It's difficult for someone to do both since their roles are dissimilar. Learn to compartmentalize and tap into others more efficiently and effectively. I've seen people share disparaging information with their advocates. That in my opinion is a no-no. An advocate must see you as toeing the party line but if you talk about the ills of the organization, can she trust that you will represent her and the company if she were to push you forward? I do believe that you should give them a heads up on any problems; however, they are not there to resolve issues. What you need to know is that you do not talk about disappointments or in short, things that shine a dim light on the company, your boss, etc. That type of information is for your mentor who may be able to help you resolve issues or, better yet, your supporter who is there to care about you and your well-being. If you recall from the first book, supporters are people such as a spouse, parents, friends and some colleagues who are there for you. Utilize people based on their appropriate role(s), in your career and life.

12. Don't Complain to Your Advocate

I know that this seems like I am repeating myself. And, maybe I am because I continue to see this as an issue and I cannot emphasize this enough. I was at a conference and mentioned this. The speaker said she would disagree because an advocate may need to know about your challenge to avoid being blindsided or to help resolve it. Let me clarify. Don't talk about how you don't like your boss, the company, etc. They must be completely confident that you are 100% drinking the organizational juice, since they are placing their reputation and possibly favors on you. If you look like you may abandon ship or cause a black eye, they will be less likely to move your name forward on things. However, I do agree that letting them know of situations is beneficial and that you should be positively transparent. But, an advocate is not there to resolve issues for you; that is a mentor, supporter or boss. Don't make someone your everything. Compartmentalize with your C.A.R.S. As discussed in my first book, C.A.R.S. is Colleagues, Advocates, Resources and Supporters; each of which plays a unique role. In short, don't become a burden to your advocate. They have more important things to do than to get wrapped up in your problems. Let them open doors, speak highly of you and advocate, not fight or troubleshoot for you. To be honest no one wants to sign up for that.

13. Separate Yourself from People Who Can Pull You Down

There are some people who believe they can save anyone and that it is their responsibility to help people reach the next level if they manage them. I believe it is your responsibility to provide the resources and opportunity for growth. If someone is not a positive influence or is seen as a problem, etc., it would behoove you to separate yourself from them. Let me use the illustration of a chair. If you are standing up on a chair which is symbolic of a higher position, status or whatever, and then there is a colleague who is standing on the ground, representative of a lower mindset, negative behavior, etc., is it easier for you to pull him up or for him to pull you down? It's difficult to pull someone up without tipping over the chair or losing your balance. There is a risk associated with helping this individual. Be mindful of risking your career for others. Remember the quote I repeated earlier that said, "I don't regret the things I did wrong. I regret the good things I did for the wrong people." When I look back at my career, I can honestly say that every failure was attached to someone whom I trusted that didn't deserve my support, help or collaboration. Although it is in my nature to give and help others, I had to become more discerning with what I do for certain people. I once helped someone who did some unethical stuff on which I called her out. When I shared with her my disappointment based on my trying to 'help' her, she candidly said, "I didn't ask for your help." Well, she did in my opinion, but I get it. She was saying that I chose to extend the type of help I gave. And, she pulled me down. I later realized for myself that I could not help someone who didn't want help. That was an uncomfortable and costly lesson learned. I now ask people whether they want my help or not. I don't assume or arbitrarily do things that I believe they will value or want me to do.

14. At Some Point, Rule in Hell as Opposed to Always Serving in Heaven

Your career will have an upward trajectory that you can't imagine when you spend some time in hell. What is meant by that is that nearly every organization has a department, division or project that no one wants to work in because there may be a myriad of issues. But think about it. If you join a professional sport team that already has a star player who plays your same position, and has gone to the championship year after year, what is the likelihood that you're going to get any playing time? What that means is you are not going to develop new skills. However, if you go to a terrible team and help them win a championship, you are the hero! Everyone will want you on their team to work your magic. If you get into a department and turn it around, you'll be seen as someone who can solve problems. The trick is to not stay too long. Staying in hell too long may cause you to become one of the demons versus the ruler. Meaning, give yourself a time frame and a goal to accomplish and plan to move on. This is about taking an assignment to build and strengthen your resume while increasing the performance of the organization. Some professionals seek to be in the best or in an easy office working on projects which can cause complacency and maybe deprive them of demonstrating their true worth. Occasionally, take those hard projects that no one wants or move into a part of the company that needs saving; be the super star or game player there. The risks may be great, but the rewards are greater. If you really care about your organization/company, see the totality of it. See how its overall success will create opportunities for you. Here's an example: look at a struggling team that hires a new coach. He brings his "A" game but the team continues to lose. Often, woefully mismanaged teams will fire that coach not understanding that it will take time to build a winning team. But, if he succeeds he can write his own ticket. What are the risks in a company? An organization may or may not be realistic in their expectations; thus, placing pressure on you to succeed. But, if you want a career with a path to top leadership or anything attached to a high salary, you should take difficult assignments. That is where you will develop knowledge, skills and abilities that will increase your stats.

15. Put Away Your Laptop and Phone at Meetings

We cannot live without our mobile devices; it has gone to the extent where some people are on them while in meetings. It can be very distracting to your peers speaking with the team, while your head is buried in your laptop or phone. When you do it to leadership, it can be disconcerting to them because they may not feel valued, respected or heard. The very thing that you want, they want. Also, you lose the opportunity to engage people. Here's a caveat: if you are one of those millennials who is always on your laptop, pull up information to support your colleagues. Then let it be known that you are online and have information that can be beneficial to the discussion. Now, that will earn you some bonus points. Otherwise, put your gadgets away and be a part of what is happening at that time: be present.

16. Be Visible

As more people work from the home or are in countries different to that of their boss or peers, they must make a concerted effort to be visible. Out of sight could lead to out of mind. If you are in the same city or when you arrive in their city, make it a point to carve out a day here and there to go in and walk around to chat with people and drop by key people's offices to just say hello and inquire about their projects, etc. to show genuine interest. Go to lunch frequently with peers who you don't see on a day-to-day basis. You need to put in some face time with your C.A.R.S. I attribute a significant part of my success to management by walking. This doesn't mean you must be a manager, but rather you manage your career by walking. I would walk by everyone's desk on the way in and say hello or briefly chat. And, I would select someone to ask to walk with me to get coffee, as I mentioned before. When I held a job, I would drop by my boss' office to poke my head in to say hello and to see if she had a minute to play catch up and to keep her in the loop. That went a long way. I would come in early to build that time into my work schedule because I saw it as a part of career management. Also, I said good night to everyone as I left for the evening.

When there are forced fun events that other employees are attending such as going out for a beer after work, make sure you show up. When working from home, kick off those fuzzy slippers and get dressed to head over to the meet up. You'll be amazed at what you are missing over time by not showing up. It really doesn't need to be said how important decisions can be made at the bar, on the golf course, etc. It is important to say that tinkering away at home working hard is not going to help you when all things are considered equal, and a decision for something comes down to you and another employee who has consistent face time with her peers and boss. All things being considered equal, visibility may be the tie breaker between you and your peers when you are going after the same promotion, project, salary increase or termination within a tight budget, etc.

17. Don't Dip Your Pen in the Company Inkwell

In short, don't have sexual relations with colleagues. The quote of all quotes regarding this matter came from past President Clinton when he ended a televised speech in late January 1998 by saying, "I did not have sexual relations with that woman, Miss Lewinsky." And, we know how that ended (wink). In some instances, they can work out well. And sometimes they don't, and when I say they don't; they don't. When a woman is dating someone at work, it is called dating. When they break it off, it is referred to as, "He was sleeping with her." Totally different connotation, right? I usually warn women of the downfall but, hey guys: what was a great relationship can become caustic when things go awry and what was consensual can become harassment. As for women, they may be demoted or reassigned when the powers that be start believing that your affair will be a distraction or a law suit waiting to happen. Yeah, this can be a slippery slope for both men and women. There's a phrase, "bedroom to boardroom," which is to leave home and go to work and back. It can be a problem for workaholics who blend their career with their personal life with no break in between the two. So, let's change the phrase slightly: don't sleep in your board room. Boardroom is for work while your bedroom is for play; don't combine the two.

18. Understand the Meaning of Time

Don't be late, but don't be too early. I lived by a saying, "When you are early, you are on time; when you are on time, you are late; and when you are late, that is unacceptable." I'm on time to a fault; so much so that I'm usually too early. I have to plan to be somewhere nearly late or on time so that I don't show up too early. In Asia, it is expected to be a little late. If I had a

10:00 am meeting I would show up at 9:30 am; thus, making whomever I was meeting nervous and even agitated. I felt so bad for showing up early that I would wait somewhere in the vicinity before walking into the building. One potential client said, "You are not on time, you are early, again." That was all that had to be said for me to change my strategy for this game. On time seemed to be five minutes within the start of the meeting time, if not exactly at the actual time of the meeting. Figure out the expectations of the company or person you are meeting to be on their time. I found that to be a huge thing in Asia. Keep in mind that most games are governed by time in terms of minutes, quarters, etc. Games can be won or lost in the span of seconds. So, learn the meaning of time and how it is regarded by the players you are playing with within the game.

19. Don't Run a Business from Your Cubicle

If you are a real-estate agent on the side, sell Mary Kay or have a gig with products or services, don't use your employer's space and time for that gig. That is totally unprofessional and quite frankly a form of stealing. I've gone into offices and seen where someone has their product lined up for purchase on their desk. Really? As an employer, I find this to be unacceptable to see when walking through organizations that I visit. I was dating this guy who brought me flowers and lunch to my company's office, one day. While sitting in my office he looked puzzled. To my knowledge, it was his first time coming to my office, but he said, "Indigo, I've been here before." I was sure he was mistaken. I had an interesting floor plan. The office had two front sides with a back area that consisted of cubicles and a printing room. My office was on the far side with a private conference room away from the main entrance. He described one of my conference rooms which was located near the front entrance and receptionist desk. He then described the person whom he had a meeting with. That employee had another gig as a consultant, and he met his clients in my office during work hours. I was flabbergasted. In my opinion, if you are a manager and you discover such egregious unethical actions, terminate that employee immediately. I didn't. Instead, I shared with his manager what had occurred and requested that he reprimand him. There is no telling what else that employee is stealing from the company. At any rate, my friend was accurate in describing a part of my office space that he hadn't seen and in describing an employee who later, presumably, stole a contract along with the manager who 'reprimanded' him. Well, that is a whole other level of unethical, but as a manager you can't play favoritism that an employee selling skin care products is different than someone who is promoting services that are based on billable hours. Yes, theoretically it is different, but both take time away from doing their actual job. That time adds up which becomes monetary loss to the company. As a professional, don't use company time for your part time gig.

20. Trust Your Instincts

We all have a voice that is our true or higher self. That voice often tells us right from wrong and speaks to us to help us make the right decisions. Unfortunately, we don't listen to that voice. We have learned that decisions made with concrete data and facts are valuable. Yet, hunches and gut instinct have made some people millions. If you feel intuitively that something isn't right, listen to that voice. Do a little digging around to find evidence to support that feeling, and don't discount it. Have you ever become lost and found yourself at an intersection; wherein, you must turn one way or another? Something tells you to go left but you don't listen, and you turn right to find yourself in a much worse situation than before. Had you turned left, you would have been back on track, but you added time and frustration to this trip. Time and time again we do this, and then that voice gently says, "I told you so." We don't listen to that still, but quiet voice and we wonder why we keep finding ourselves in situations that cause us to lose focus on more important matters.

21. Manage Your Brand

There are workshops that speak to the importance of a personal brand, especially with social media. Manage your image and how others perceive you based on what you put out there. As for the brand, know your story and what people say about you based on what you put out there. Every now and then Google yourself. If there is absolutely nothing out there, you need to create a visible footprint. But, more importantly, remember that absolutely everything that you put out there will stay out there! My son who is in college and wants to be in the movie industry loves commenting on things, tweeting, and sharing his opinions online. I told him to be careful because what he believes strongly today may not be what he advocates in the future and someone may pull up some old quote and challenge him on it when he attains a level of success that may cause people to come after him. Don't create your image just for today but think about the future of your career. Decide what will be your legacy and allow that to guide your conversations, online image, etc.

22. Don't Speak of Politics

It's funny how people assume that you will support one candidate or another based on your gender, ethnicity, race, etc. This then leads them into a false sense of familiarity; whereby, they start spouting off their views and opinions because they think both of you have a kindred spirit. Oh contraire. That person may hate your candidate and thus resents hearing about your misplaced support. Case in point, my brother who happens to be an African American sharing the same mom and dad as me might cause people to think we have the same views. I voted for President Obama while my brother voted Republican. He has that right. So here is the point: he is a supervisor on the police force. Another police officer could be making a serious mistake telling my brother how the Republican Party is filled with idiots and that anyone who votes for that party is an idiot, as well. But, people who vote along the Democratic party line may assume that my brother shares their views based on historical data that shows 88% of Black Americans vote for Democrats. This may give someone who is a Democrat a misplaced confidence that he can espouse his views and opinions with my brother. Now, you may be saying, "No one would be that dumb." Yes, not just someone, many people make this mistake. Now, you may not put down one candidate over another based on a stereotype or assumed beliefs, but you may join in on a conversation with someone who shares your belief. However, you never know who is eavesdropping or how your comrade may use that information. You may be sharing a moment where you are going hard about some practices that you both feel are unjust. All is well and fine until that comrade is in a heated debate with another colleague and he states his case by using you as someone who agrees and endorses his belief. He says something like, "Yeah. Well Randy and I were talking, and Randy said that xyz is probably one of the worst administrations for people of color and I tend to agree with him." What? Did Randy just get thrown under the bus by a colleague who was merely trying to make a point using Randy's credibility? It's somewhat of a compliment that Randy's word has value to him, but a slap in the face that Randy may be at the center of someone's annoyance and he isn't even there to defend what was said. Just one of the many ways a train can go off the tracks, real fast.

23. Don't Use the Company's Credit Card for Anything Other Than Company Business

Okay, do I really need to address this? The employee handbook clearly states this, but people get around it by saying they are having lunch with their peers and/or they are talking about work. That is unethical and once again stealing. Buy your own lunch unless you are with a client; not a colleague.

24. Don't Upstage Others, Unnecessarily

At engagements, I give people the rules for asking or responding to a question. It is the 4-Ss: Stand-up, Speak up, Shut up, and Sit down. I sometimes find people will want to steal the show or demonstrate their wealth of knowledge at the expense of other people's time. I loved how Oprah would never let people take her mic when she went out into the audience on the Oprah Show. I guess she knew that people would talk until she had to cut to a commercial. There is always a time and place to disagree, debate or simply expound upon your thoughts. The worst time is when senior leadership is speaking, especially if it is a monologue and not a dialogue. Tread lightly; don't spout off what you think and believe. That is best done up close and personal. But, if you really have a question, need clarification or want to bring attention to something, I recommend brevity. And, don't use a public venue for a private conversation.

25. When in a Position to Change Things, Change Things

Some people try to change things when they have neither the power nor influence, which can prove to be disastrous. And then some do not attempt to change things once they have the power and influence. If you played the game and there were rules that you encountered that were unfair, unreasonable, etc. then change it for those coming behind you. Don't perpetuate what was difficult for you or that you see as unjust just because you had to. I hear people say things like "I had to do it." What? Yeah, changing the game is nobler than playing the game. As I listed reasons for unwritten rules in the previous book, sometimes the rules are preferential. So, as we move up the ladder of success, we will create rules that accommodate our style of managing or leading, but be mindful that for you to bring out the best in people, you have to allow people to show up with some level of authenticity. What this means is that we have to occasionally allow people to be their whole self, and that's tough. I learned the hard way as a leader. It can't be solely about you if you want people to perform and be at their best. That is a general rule.

26. Follow Up on Support

Within one week, I had two friends share with me that they were in dire straits and needed a job. One said that she wanted an admin position since she had been out of the workplace for a while, the other friend lost her job and would take anything to keep the lights on. A dear colleague had a job that would allow someone to work from home doing light admin work. I explained the opportunity to both my friends, referred them both and let my colleague know that she would be getting a call based on them saying that they would follow up. I reached into my network to support them. They said that they would call the woman. Not once, not twice did I ask the two friends if they contacted my colleague. Days passed, and no call was made by either friend. I was a little annoyed because I reached into my network and offered something that I did not deliver on. I've spoken to each person and there was not an explanation or discussion about them not following up. I will not make the mistake of opening my network to them, again. Professionals hold their network, reputation and image in high regard. When people refer you, that is saying that they believe that you meet the criteria and that they support/advocate for you. What should have happened is that they called or emailed my contact, asked a few questions and simply stated that it was not a fit. That is better than no response even though no response, is a response (an unprofessional one). Now, some may say, just tell them flat out that you aren't interested and don't waste either of your time. Well, that makes the person who referred you look bad by seeming to be ill-informed and it makes you look bad by not even allowing the person to share what they believe is important. What harm will it do to take a few minutes to listen and then let them know whatever you think. You may want what they have to offer after all or, they may consider you for something else or refer you within their network.

This Is What I Know

This is not a full list of unwritten rules and it doesn't represent some/all rules for some/all companies. However, when you combine all three of my books in this series, you have a comprehensive list with 15 unwritten rules from the first book and 24 unwritten rules from the second book. Aside from a list of unwritten rules, I've shared with you suggested tips, techniques and methods for playing the game. But, it is incumbent upon you to learn your organization's unwritten rules. Also, understand that the rules change with time. Many years ago, I would spend an inordinate amount of time arguing with women about the importance of wearing stockings. Some hated wearing stockings, but I would keep telling them that if senior executive men were wearing stockings then they needed to follow suit. I would give the example that stockings are like socks for men. Could men show up with business shoes and no socks? I even went so far as to speak about how women needed to wear shoes and not sandals, etc. But, now things are less conservative, and women are wearing mules, slings, open toed shoes, and more. Times have changed. I'm in a very hot climate. I don't wear stockings, not even on the stage where I'm supposed to be polished. It's appropriate now and it fits the new culture of what is business professional.

You must take things into consideration. At the end of the day, you must figure out what make sense and what applies in your industry and organization. If you see that something is a common practice and you choose not to do it, the issue is less about the game and more about your ego. There is a difference between ego and doing what is called playing the game. Some people refuse to do something because of misplaced pride or they listen to their ego which doesn't work for their highest good. If you are ever in doubt, listen to your inner voice. There is a small still voice that speaks to us. It will say, "Just do it," while the ego is saying, "You don't have to put up with that." Step back and think about the situation.

I had a woman share with me that she didn't particularly like her boss, but that he stands between her and a promotion. I asked, "What is your inner voice telling you? She said, "It is saying that I shouldn't have to appease him." I looked at her with empathy and said, "That is ego talking," while shaking my head slowly. I simply told her that an unwritten rule is to know what makes your boss tick and what ticks him off. She said that she knew exactly what made him tick and vice versa. I asked her if she did things that made him tick. She responded with defiance, "No, because I don't feel that I should have to." Again, that is the ego talking. If you want what he has or can give, you need to give him what he wants that you can give. If compliments make him tick, then give them. If completing assignments early makes his day, complete assignments early. If coming in a little early makes him tick, come in a little early and make sure he knows it. That is the stupid game that some people are too smart to play and then, they can't understand why they aren't getting what they want. Tuck your ego in your backpack, briefcase or purse and listen to the quiet voice that tells you to laugh at his jokes, etc. What else can I say? We make choices. I'm pleased that I've laughed at some jokes that made someone feel valued when I could have looked at them like a deer in the head lights. What would I have gained, but more importantly what would I have lost? If what you are doing doesn't go against your integrity, authenticity, character, spirit and so forth, then choose to do that which will create a sustainable career, while allowing others to feel valued. What's wrong with that? Or rather, what's wrong with people? These are the types of conversations that I have following each of my presentations and it's exhausting.

Lastly, remember that this is all about choices, right? I had a woman and a guy walk out of one of my sessions angry about my choices and the fact that I emphasized that we make choices. To be honest, I think they wanted to hook up. No seriously, you had to watch it unfold. They were like monkeys in a hot Volkswagen when I told the pink versus purple shirt story. They fed off each other's negativity. The woman jumped on that story and said that she wouldn't have wanted the job or contract if she couldn't be herself. Let's be real. I already owned the purple shirt. So, it wasn't a stretch. And, it didn't offend my sensibility or spirit. People have become so individualistic that they fight the wrong fight. I wasn't going to lose sleep or feel less than genuine for selecting a color that will make a boardroom filled with men feel more comfortable with me. Heck a guy could be pitching for the same contract and wear a pink shirt, and no one would bat an eye. But these darn rules have several meanings for different people. I can choose to be "me" and run the risk of not getting something I want, or I can play the damn game. I choose to play the game and, by the way, I play to win.

I believe that you should be what the company needs and pays for from 9 am to 5 pm and I can be whatever I want to be from 5 pm till 9 am. I'm okay with that. She wasn't and walked out and took a guy who supposedly felt the same way. Interestingly, neither of them were business owners. They were employees and I suspect that they have not fared well in the game or they work really hard versus really smart. I think thou protests too much. And, I'll say it again…people are hired for what they do and fired for who they are. If you are unwilling to become what a company needs you to be, then you may not acquire what you want.

I jokingly tell people that as a black woman they may assume that I have full lips because I'm black. Oh no…I have big lips because I have kissed a lot of butts. My lips are swollen. I don't have one boss, I have many bosses as an entrepreneur and the bigger the contracts the more bending and accommodating I find that I must do to keep clients who think they are more important than all others. That requires what I refer to as 'kissing butt'. But, you know what? I've had my butt kissed and those who did it knew it was part of the game. I sometimes ask things of companies, vendors, etc. that I'm sure they don't want to do, but they want my business. I guess the net net is whether you are in the right place. I liken people to seeds and companies to soil. Ask yourself if you are planted in the right soil. If you are, you don't mind the manure that will come your way some days. The manure is actually fertilization to make things grow despite how it looks and smell.

When deciding what you will and will not do, use a simple rule of thumb. Is what is being required or expected of you going against your grain, spirit or integrity? Are you simply being stubborn or is there validity to why you cannot do something? I have done some things that I didn't want to do, but I knew that it was a part of the path that I chose. I can say with pride and openness that I have never stolen, cheated or manipulated to earn what I've achieved. I may have chosen something over being with my children, I may have separated myself from someone when I should have pulled them in and so forth. But, again everything was either a lesson learnt or a learning opportunity. Therefore, I can sleep at night.

Recently, I declined an offer to work on a contract with a client because the person whom I would report to didn't show me the level of respect that I believe that I warrant, and I didn't feel valued or understood. It could have been a decent contract, but I am at a place in my career where I can turn down work and walk away. Again, I choose what I am willing and unwilling to accept, but there are consequences to all my decisions. I'm playing a new game at a higher level, which goes to say that the game shifts, the players change, but the game continues to exist, but with different rules. It took years to get here, so don't be dismayed, everything comes in due time. So, pace yourself depending on where you are in your career. This game isn't a 200-meter sprint but more like a cross country race. You may have to put up with some things while other things may be deal breakers. That's where self-awareness comes into play.

Chapter 3

Resilience: Weathering Your Storm

Why is there so much talk about resiliency these days? It could be that we are living the tale of two cities. The middle class seems to be disappearing, our government is truly divided, teens are at risk more than ever before, death by cop is on the rise and the list goes on and on, at least in America. Senselessness is popping off all over the world like movie theater popcorn. Poverty is increasing, suicide is becoming more common, and discrimination is still practiced and condoned on the glocal (global/local) stage. People keep hoping the cavalry will show up. But, unfortunately, we (you and I) are the cavalry in most situations. We gotta show up for ourselves. We are being called to truly fight for ourselves when it comes to equality, justice, rights, etc., in life in general and in the workplace. We can't solve tomorrow's problems with yesterday's solutions and antidotes. Yes, you can use tried and true medicines for what ails you today, but the strains of problems are much stronger, bigger and resistant to past solutions. Many problems need stronger remedies than what is on the shelf, which I write extensively about in the second book dealing with thinking skills. When we consider this line of thinking which is having original thought and challenging the status quo, it will require a new set of skills, knowledge and abilities for being resilient.

It seems that we are turning back the hands of time instead of progressing as people. Thus, more and more people are checking out and it's not with LSD, as they did in the 1960s. People are just tired. So, they are calling in sick for work, hitting the bars, self-medicating, and doing whatever allows them to avoid dealing with whatever ails them. This means people need to get a shot of resiliency. They have to work on bouncing back. What's the difference between people who have given up and those who are considered resilient? Resilient people utilize their skills and strengths to cope and recover from problems and challenges, which may include job loss, financial problems, illness, natural disasters, heart break and more while others give up and throw in the proverbial towel. The resilient get back up when they get knocked down, and they get back up when they get knocked back down again, again and again. It's a continuation of getting back up, time and time again.

Exercise:

List situations that had a negative impact on you, whether they stemmed from disappointment, hurt, shame, embarrassment, anger, etc. You may pull things from as far back as childhood to adulthood, both personally and professionally. Describe the situation and how it made you feel. Now, describe the impact that it had on you, specifically. Write whether you were able to overcome it or is it still a source of discomfort? Now use a highlighter to identify those things listed that occasionally or often enter your thoughts. Write down whether there are emotions attached and whether they continue to impact you in any way. Now, continue reading the chapter on what to do with those things that are lingering.

This chapter will be an opportunity to explore what you have just highlighted and figure out how to minimize the impact. As the foundation of a client's coaching session, I shared a quote from Margaret Thatcher, "Sometimes you have to fight the good fight twice." During my presentations, I show the picture of Muhammad Ali and I ask the audience if he is considered the greatest fighter of all time. Many will say yes. I'll then show a picture of him in the ring on the mat/floor down for the count. No one really speaks of his failures because he always got back up and got back in the ring. That is resilience. Resilience doesn't mean you will not fail; it means you certainly will fall, but it is what you do in those instances that will reveal whether you are resilient or not.

If you don't receive the long-awaited promotion that you were told you would get from working your butt off, you'll need resiliency. When your brand is ruined because of a lie that a competitor told, or your reputation is tarnished from a mistake that maybe you or someone else made, then you will need resiliency. Or, on a personal matter that directly impacts your career, such as getting a divorce - whether a woman or man - and your lifestyle changes, which places pressure on you to earn more, you will need to be resilient. The loss of a child, parent or anyone whom you loved requires resilience. There are numerous reasons that will call you to be resilient. If you take a moment and write down what keeps you awake at night, whatever you wrote will require resilience, especially if it does not work out in your favor or as you have planned.

Circumstances that require resilience can range from minor to catastrophic.

I had four pages discussing resiliency in the second *Playing by the Unwritten Rules* book. Interestingly, it is those four pages which people often ask me to speak about as a topic at conferences. Yes, four pages out of hundreds of pages that cover a litany of topics; and people hone in on resilience. So, what is this elusive and mysterious thing called resilience? The dictionary defines it as "The capacity to recover quickly from difficulties; toughness." It's a simple and easy thing to define but far more difficult to achieve if you have not built up your resiliency muscles. Similar to weight training, you will be able to lift heavier weights the more you lift, but in lifting those weights you will acquire scars which lead to muscles. I can't resist; here is the physiology of muscle growth to make sense of resilience: after you work out, your body repairs or replaces damaged muscle fibers through a cellular process where it fuses muscle fibers together to form new muscle protein strands or myofibrils. These repaired myofibrils increase in thickness and number to create muscle hypertrophy (growth). This is how muscle growth is explained when I Googled this information while writing this book. Resilience is the same in nature. When you encounter a tough situation and go through it, you will develop scars, but those scars become muscles to prepare you for the next negative encounter. You become more and more resilient the more you move through things, versus avoiding or not dealing with them. Resilience is not to be confused with resistance. We can use the example of a flu virus, of which there are several strains; you can be inoculated to resist one strain of the virus but not all of them. But, to be resilient is to catch the flu and recover. There is no resistance to tough times and no inoculation to protect you from the negative things that await you, despite your best efforts. Life will throw you a curve ball. Everyone will encounter problems, challenges, obstacles, disappointments and maybe even tragedy. One aspect of finding peace and joy is based on how you deal with those things, move beyond them and maybe even improve as a result of them.

I've always been resilient and often I'm characterized as a strong black woman. On dating sites, I often write in my profile, "If you like your women like your coffee: strong, black and with a little sweetness, then I'm your girl." I've come to accept that I am strong and that is based on my ability to be resilient. For years, I resented being strong because superwomen/men don't receive compassion or empathy, in my opinion. People assume that you can take whatever is thrown at you. Once I was going through some difficulties in life. Now, get this, a friend called me: I didn't call this friend because I was trying to deal with a personal matter privately. Often, I would isolate myself when going through difficulties to deal with things alone. I found that I could move faster alone when trekking through hell; however, now I have learned that there is strength in numbers. But, this friend called and after telling me about his world, he asked me how I was doing. Things must have been pretty bad because I shared that I was having a challenging time. I rarely divulge things when times are bad; I'm protective of my stuff. To be honest, most people aren't interested in your problems. But, that's my opinion. He stopped me and literally told me that he couldn't handle it. He said, "Indigo, you gotta be strong. You are strong. You'll be fine. If you go down, we all go down because you are our shoulder and rock. If you can't handle this, what does that say about us?" I was furious as I thought to myself, "Are you *%#& kidding me? This is not about you." Damn it, man! Where do super heroes go when they need a shoulder, right? But, I get it. Some people cannot deal with seeing weakness in people who they perceive as invincible or strong. Allow me to share one other example since I'm in a tell all mood. Years later, when things were falling apart with my company, an employee walked into my office to see me. I had my back turned and didn't hear her. Now, the common thread is that I did not go to anyone for support or sympathy, right? They came to me or into my space. So, I turned around when she made her presence known. She could see that I had been crying. She asked me what was wrong. I shared with her some issues that I was encountering with the company. Now, sit down for this part. She looked at me and said, "Indigo. I can't feel sorry for you. You have it all. You are intelligent, beautiful, nice family, rich and I mean you have it all," comparing her life to mine. I was stunned. I gave a gentle smile (as some women do when shocked) and just looked at her as she left my office. Damn it, man! Many months or maybe a year later when she became ill and needed special considerations and support, I supported her as an employer. She came back to work and within time, she made her way to my office. She began to speak with tears in her eyes, she thanked me for supporting her. While thanking me she apologized for what she had said many many months prior and her inability to support me. She explained that she didn't know how to be strong for me and that she felt that I could handle anything because of my strength. I resented her and people who could not and would not empathize or sympathize with me. I have since learned that 'expectation is premeditated resentment'. In short, I expected from others what I gave but did not receive in return. But, what I now know is that everyone is not designed to shoulder other people's burden; they can barely handle their own problems. So, I no longer expect it; thus, I no longer resent them or me for my strength. For many years, resentment about being strong has rode in the passenger seat with me as I drove down life's highway. I now embrace my strength because it is a part of being resilient. As you will read a little later in the book, I've been able to bounce back but not always able to let things go, which often depleted my energy to fight the good fight. But for now, let's just explore the meaning of resilience.

Even though I've been naturally resilient, it wasn't on my radar as something to be or to acquire. My first introduction to resilience was when I was attending the Tuck School of Business at Dartmouth. A professor walked into the classroom and headed straight to the dry erase board and wrote RQ. As I wrote in my first book, everyone in the classroom looked around wondering what RQ meant. We hadn't seen it in it textbooks up to that point, we didn't talk about it at conferences, and it wasn't discussed in forums that attracted business owners. So, what was the formula or acronym RQ? He explained that it was Resilience Quotient. RQ is similar to EQ, short for Emotional Quotient, which is your ability to understand others, i.e. read other people's signals and react/respond appropriately to them. In the 90s, EQ was mainstream, while IQ was popularized in the 1920s to 30s in the USA. IQ is "Intelligence quotient is a total score derived from several standardized tests designed to assess human intelligence" according to Wikipedia. It is not a fair or accurate way to determine intelligence because it doesn't take into account culture, exposure, the fact that some people are not good test takers and that it is extremely biased. What HR practitioners and leaders have discovered is that it certainly does not demonstrate one's ability to be a success; which is why EQ was embraced. At this point, RQ seems to be the new EQ, which replaced IQ in the workplace. You can be intelligent but lack the ability to inspire or motivate people as a leader, which will make you an ineffective leader or employee, for that matter. If you have EQ but collapse when hard times hit, you will again be an ineffective leader. Maybe a combination of intelligence (true intelligence not test scores), emotional acuity and resilience are truly what is needed for career success. Let's continue to focus on the importance of resilience.

Technology has changed the world in terms of giving us immediate access to information that can fuel intelligence, and there is less and less workplace interaction, which allows some people to escape the need for being able to tap into others, now that we are in the digital era. I believe introverts, i.e. computer geeks, keep designing ways to function in the world without having to engage and interact with others because they are inept in communication as communicators. To some extent, we may be able to get through a day or two without engaging others, but the one thing we cannot seem to avoid is the need to deal with hardship, disappointment, etc. There's no app or program for that. So, RQ is the new way for now to determine your capacity for sustainable success.

Chapter 3: Resilience: Weathering Your Storm

So, what does this mean? I've shared with audiences that you are either going into a storm, in a storm or coming out of a storm. I experienced in the last four years the PERFECT STORM! Of course, I Googled *Perfect Storm* and found that it is a true meteorological phenomenon that happens infrequently. According to Wikipedia, "A 'perfect storm' is an expression that describes an event where a rare combination of circumstances will aggravate a situation drastically. [1] The term is also used to describe an actual phenomenon that happens to occur in such a confluence, resulting in an event of unusual magnitude."

So, *The Perfect Storm* is not just a Hollywood blockbuster hit starring George Clooney. It's not one storm, but rather a few storms that come together at one time. Career wise, it is a particularly bad or critical state of affairs, arising from a number of negative and unpredictable factors. To bring meaning and context to this chapter, allow me to share with you a perfect storm that I encountered that required forgiveness and letting go to save my life, mind and spirit. It's not necessary but it would be very beneficial if you read or re-read the "Resilience" chapter in *Playing by the Unwritten Rules: From a Job Defense to a Career Offense* which is the second book of this series. It gives you a foundation about resiliency and why that is important. But, that was written before my perfect storm, so this gives clarity on what facilitates resiliency. If you recall, a perfect storm is the combination of storms, and here are three storms that I have encountered over a four-year period:

Storm 1:   The Divorce: Cheaper to Keep Him

I should have taken to heart the lyrics from the 1970's hit single, "Cheaper to Keep Her," by Johnnie Taylor. Nearly four years ago, I asked my then-husband for a divorce. He worked for me as my Chief Financial Officer; therefore, he knew how much the contracts that my company held were worth and how much I earned. I felt extorted when he gave me the option of him taking half my business or my giving him ½-million US dollars, in addition to the house with all the furniture, custody of our youngest son, child support, a time share and miscellaneous stuff. By law, he had the legal rights to my company because of the laws within the State that we lived. Supposedly, the courts assume that everything should be split down the middle. It is believed that married couples acquire things jointly. But, my wasband (was my husband = wasband) had a mortgage business that was on life support before joining my company because of the housing collapse of 2008. We built our companies separately. When he came on board to my company, I had earned my first multi-million dollar contract and I paid him more than he had ever earned in his career. As my lawyer explained, the laws of half were designed for women homemakers whose husbands left them for the secretary during a time when most wives were stay-at-home moms. The laws were designed to protect them and help them get on their feet after a divorce. It wasn't designed for a self-sufficient man with an MBA who had served as a Marine Corps Officer and had every credential imaginable to allow him to land on his feet. But, I had more than him, so he could reach his hands into my side of things; thus, the half. He knew all about my finances and used that to his advantage. Regretfully, I agreed to his terms and paid him the money. He left my company and went back to his mortgage company under a contract to oversee my finances and continue to provide technical support for my business, which lasted a few months. I then moved some people into new positions to fill the gaps caused by his departure.

I lost my marriage of 23 years by choice, but it was still a loss. I lost my best friend: my wasband who was my best friend. I lost a significant amount of my money. But, the greatest loss was the ideal future of having a home where the grandchildren would come and watch me bake cookies, we'd all laugh around the holiday table, and just shower each other with love and be loved. That was gone; the ideal family that I had worked at constructing within a 23-year-old marriage while building my business vanished in the court room. Sometimes, it isn't what we actually lose but the ideal, the fantasy that we construct that is difficult to part with. In truth, I gave up a cell mate to be available for my soul-mate, should he exist. But, the entire divorce journey was expensive in many ways. I now know that freedom ain't free.

Storm 2:   Tammy Gate: Betrayal and Intrigue

The one true constant in my business, and essentially my career was my most trusted and faithful confidant Tamara Wright Mulliro Davis Carter (a woman of many names and faces). She had been with my company for many years and grew as the company grew. I trusted and loved her like a daughter. I took a special interest in her and her family, and I would do many things to support her, primarily because she supported me personally and professionally. There was nothing that I would ask of her that she didn't do. She treated my company as if it were her company; what more could you ask of someone? It was a symbiotic relationship, so, I rewarded her well and provided resources to support her and her family, as she was a single mom for most of her employment with my company. I think what really pulled on my heart strings is that she had beaten cancer many years ago, while working for my company, but it came back. I was giving her a lot of time off for doctors' appointments, chemotherapy and healing.

A few years ago, I was audited by the IRS and it was resolved based on her efforts. The company began experiencing difficulties, which I couldn't understand. At that time, her cancer returned, and I started getting hit hard by the IRS again, and whenever we were supposed to meet with my CPA and the IRS agent to go over accounts, etc., she kept missing appointments for reasons ranging from being too sick to a car accident blocking all the lanes preventing her from attending a meeting. All the while, my company was experiencing a slow death that didn't completely make sense. I attributed it to the money I was paying my wasband, the completion of a major multi-million dollar contract, a suit I brought against a partner, and the retirement of several key clients. I believed the financial difficulties were a result of the occasional ebb and flow of a 20+ year old company. I've had lean and mean times, but I couldn't understand what was happening. However, I was confident that we would be fine. We just needed to weather the storm (wink). But, things got progressively worse, and I had to call my wasband who had previously managed Tammy. He knew the various passwords to her computer and my accounting books. I asked him to come to my office to help me get my finances ready for the IRS, which was Tammy's job, but she was missing in action, right? He pulled up my company's QuickBooks accounts which was on one of Tammy's computers and turned to me and said with confusion, "There is nothing here. She hasn't done your books in nearly a year." I assured him that he was wrong because she kept everything up to date. He shockingly waved me over, and said, "See for yourself." I didn't understand what I was looking at, but he explained to me what was right before my eyes. Tammy was not keeping my books. So, I had to hire a company that had provided similar services in the past. Ironically, this company was scheduled to conduct an audit a year prior, but Tammy convinced me that we couldn't afford it based on the losses we were incurring.

Well, the CPA within that company that I hired on a short-term contract came in and brought my books up to date so that I could turn everything over to my company's CPA. That is when she uncovered that Tammy had paid herself an additional six figures through pay roll. Then we started seeing vendors and consultants that I didn't recognize earning anything from $1,000 to $32,000, frequently and consistently. And, there were discrepancies after discrepancies that were identified. We discovered that she had embezzled over half-a-million dollars through money and damages over a two-year period. In short, since my wasband left and she had complete control and access to payroll, she moved money into her and other people's accounts.

To make a long story short, there was an uphill battle to prove it to the police but after six months of sending proof, meeting with investigators and complaining that justice wasn't being served, she was finally arrested. She was released on bond and I am still going through the process of a criminal case. The District Attorney's investigator found 12 accounts into which she funneled money. At this moment in time, money and damages have surpassed $1 million dollars, as opposed to a Final Order which was a judgement for $717,307.53 that I was awarded by the Superior Court of Rockdale County, Georgia in a civil suit against Tamara Wright Carter. Hmmm, I've been awarded close to one million dollars that I may never see (sigh). Oh, by the way, did I mention that she didn't have cancer? That was a lie to defraud me. If you recall, I mentioned earlier that she worked from home because she was battling cancer. Instead of healing and resting, she used my money to start a business. She used my company's slogan for her company's name and she used my company's money to finance it. Many people lost their job, I lost nearly everything from my money to my emotional well-being and she ruined my company. I found pictures and documents retrieved from the network that showed identity theft, but what was most shocking is that she did things that mirrored my life, too. This was truly an imitation of life.

At any rate, the criminal investigation revealed that she had a co-conspirator. She and a senior leader within my company were in cahoots. Not only did this person commit fraud and payroll theft, but this guy started a competing business too and stole one of my company's lucrative contracts. Before I had this information about the entire embezzlement and their collaboration, I attempted to sue this prior employee, but Tammy pretended to be unable to find his contract or employee records to prove breach of contract. He got off the hook, but, I was able to sue the company that partnered with him in stealing the contract and we settled out of court for a monthly sum.

Anyhow, I basically lost everything that I felt was of value because I had to terminate a contract and let go of employees based on cash flow problems caused by her theft. My business went on life support because of all the liens and judgements placed on my company based on her redirecting money into dummy accounts, i.e., her 12 bank accounts, and to her friends and family, as opposed to paying my company's bills. I couldn't even rent an apartment because my credit was destroyed, presumably because she used my identity to get and use credit cards that went into default. As you may or may not know, credit is the financial life blood of America. I then decided that I would take what I had left and find somewhere to start all over. I was basically homeless.

It was a tossup between Central America and Asia. I selected Asia. With my life in shambles, I left all that I knew and loved in the US. For three years, I fought for her indictment by working closely with law enforcement, investigators, attorneys, banks, accountants and others throughout each night because of the time difference between the US and Asia. It paid off because the criminal investigation proved embezzlement. At this point, it's a matter of what happens with an indictment to seek criminal charges and possible jail time. The saga continues.

Storm 3:   Give Me Justice or Give Me Death

After three months of being in Asia, I nearly died twice. This would be the third storm, although so much more happened that I am unable to write about in this book. Now, remember: a perfect storm is a combination of significant storms that wreak havoc and destroy anything in its path. Before I left for Asia, I had to get an emergency blood transfusion and then I boarded an overseas flight two days later. I never experienced needing a blood transfusion, and I had no idea how ill I had become over time. I thought it was merely a fluke and that whatever was causing that problem would work itself out. But, I was under a tremendous amount of stress, from pushing to get Tammy arrested to trying to sort out my life that had unraveled at the seams. I came to Asia in September with 10 boxes of personal items to help me get on my feet and my middle son who accompanied me. In December, I took a trip back to the US to deal with the ongoing investigation and other dire and burdensome business matters. I had been complaining of leg pain and swelling since my arrival to Asia, but it had gotten worse. I tried to stretch my legs as much as possible and wore compression stocking during the flight. Upon landing in Chicago, I stepped outside and started coughing uncontrollably. It was the weirdest thing. I assumed that I caught the flu on the 24-hour journey combined with the bitter coldness of the Midwest. I shrugged it off. My family bought me many over the counter remedies for flu and cough. Nothing worked. I then made my way down south to visit my mom. She tried different things as well to help my cough subside. And, my leg was throbbing, too. After a couple of weeks with my health deteriorating, I headed back to Asia. I was in so much pain that I Googled, what can cause excruciating leg pain? It felt like what I imagined cancer to feel like if cancer had a feeling, right? A website listed about 10 ailments with possible problems. I saw one ailment that suggested that if leg pain was accompanied with coughing, I needed to seek medical attention immediately. I woke up my middle son and said, "I think that I may have a problem and need to go to the hospital." He called the hospital which directed him to take me to the emergency room. Being an American, I thought that I couldn't afford the emergency room because the cost would be exorbitant. So, he made an appointment for me later that day, and took me in for a routine checkup. I was seen by several specialists that afternoon. I was diagnosed with Deep Vein Thrombosis (DVT) and Pulmonary Embolism (PE). I read that over 60% of cases are diagnosed through autopsy versus someone coming to the hospital with complications. People simply die on the airplane, drop dead walking somewhere or there are complications from surgery. My doctor said that I should have died when I reached America and started coughing; but the blood clots passed through my heart avoiding a heart attack. Then all the additional travel should have killed me from either an aneurism or stroke, due to all the blood clots deposited in my lungs that could have become dislodged. So, that was the first near death experience.

The second near death experience was about two weeks later, I began to hemorrhage and bleed out. They could not stop the bleeding, which created other problems. The blood thinner Xarelto did its job but it was killing me. A hematologist, gynecologist and cardiologist literally stood by my hospital bed and debated on how to save my life. They each had what was their area of expertise, but what one doctor would recommend would cause concern for the other doctor. For example, the gynecologist said, "I can give her something to clot the blood which will slow down or stop the bleeding." The cardiologist said, "That can cause a heart attack." The hematologist interrupted and said, "We have to do something or she's going to bleed to death." Then they realized that I was laying there listening. They left my room to have some privacy while they pow wowed. My primary doctor returned and placed his hand on my shoulder and assured me that they would figure something out.

I just wanted it over. Each night became an exhausting death watch, as I prepared to die. I made all the preparations from my hospital bed, ranging from making my son my financial trustee to selecting the perfect music for my memorial. Yet, I lived. It took over six months to recuperate, but I'm alive. Hmmm, maybe give me justice or give me death is a little melodramatic for any cause. I thought that I wanted to die after I lost nearly everything, until death sat at the foot of my bed. Now, I realize how precious life is and to live with intentionality and purpose.

I spared you the details on each storm. There are many twists and turns that I don't have time or space to discuss, but this lays the foundation for this chapter and subsequent chapters.

As I write, the investigation has ended, and the District Attorney is moving to an indictment where they may seek three to 10 years as a prison sentence if Tammy is convicted. To say the least, the last four years have been tumultuous and that doesn't include rain showers between the thunderstorms. There are other things that have occurred, but these are the main forces that created the perfect storm.

No one teaches us how to be resilient. I believe that I am resilient based on where I was raised, to whom I was born, and what circumstances I've encountered from a child up until now. Resiliency is something you build up over time. Each situation prepares you for future unfavorable encounters.

My middle son and I have debated much about his generation and mine. I believe many young adults such as Generation X, Gen Y and Millennials are not as resilient. He adamantly disagrees. I tend to think that they haven't had to encounter the same level of hardship as their parents or their parents' parents. We parents have shielded and protected them from many storms that could have given them a foundation and the scars to build resilience muscles. I will say that they are often courageous about speaking up and fighting for their rights, yet I'm not too sure that they have encountered things like those that forced traditionalists and baby boomers to become resilient. This is not to discredit or slight younger professionals, but I want everyone to consider their level of resilience. Also, keep in perspective the Bell Curve Theory. There's a small percentage of them who have fought in wars, experienced neglect, survived natural disasters, etc., but the majority of them have been shielded from harm.

Similar to the flu, the strains (problems) get stronger and our immune systems (resilience) seem to be getting weaker. My grandparents went through World Wars, civil unrest, the not so great great depression, etc. But, overall, my children have had it relatively easy. So, when they meet problems, they easily crumble. Society didn't allow us to put pressure on them the way we were challenged. I don't think I'm doing a decent job at articulating this. But, what I'm trying to say about younger professionals is that, based on time and exposure, they have not been tasked to deal with things that life will bring to their doorstep at any given time; they've been sheltered, protected and supported by parents far more differently from how seasoned professionals were raised. So, it may be less about generations and more about time. Each one of us has and will encounter our own storms. Interestingly, what is a storm for one person may be a cloudy day for someone else. I lost everything of value to me; at least, I thought those things were of value, right? I nearly gave up and died because of the hate and rage that consumed me, but I had to get up, brush myself off and start swinging to fight back. Someone else may be encountering something that they feel is far more significant. Regardless of what you perceive as a storm or not, it is relative. You must be resilient to whatever shows up at your door. So, that was what I think, and here is what I know:

1. **Time is Relative**

    Time is neither a determining factor on the impact of a storm nor when it will end. A tornado can blow through quickly and take an entire town with it, while thunder showers can pour for days and cause flash floods. My storm has been hovering over me for four years with moments of clear skies and then darkness all over again, while your storm can be four hours of sheer panic. Don't use time as a way to validate or dismiss how you feel. You can be deeply affected, so don't down play your situation or someone else's based on time.

2. **Trust and Believe That You are Going to Come Out of the Storm**

    Know that every storm will pass. Unfortunately, when things are at their darkest and the clouds seem to hover within inches of your head, you can't imagine the sunshine. But, if you look past the gloominess you can envision that just over the dark clouds the sky is clear. Think about how a plane will take off in terrible conditions, but once it breaks through the clouds, it is bright and sunny. So, believe that you will come through it because you will! Storms will always pass. I think the most difficult part of being in a storm is the eye of the storm when things seem to be okay and then it is pitch dark again. It's okay… you are moving through the storm.

3. **Acknowledge Your Reality**

    Some people will tell you that what you are going through is not as bad as it seems. First, they don't know what the *%># they are talking about because they cannot get into your mind or heart to assess how something is truly impacting you. They can only use their own frame of reference. So, acknowledge your reality in terms of recognizing what you feel is real and don't allow others to define what is or is not significant. This is your stuff, so handle it.

4. **Keep Moving**

    When going through hell, don't stop: keep moving forward! Don't turn around, because you already know what is back there; just keep moving forward, and preferably with people who will support you and move with you. Looking back can be compared to driving your car down the road and looking in your rearview mirror to figure out where you are going. You'll see where you've been, but it won't prepare you completely for what is ahead. It will give you some insight but not enough to get you to wherever you are going safely. So, look back to assess what the heck happened or is happening to understand where you've been, and then look forward as you keep moving.

5. **Become Aware**

   Resilient people are aware of their situation, their own emotional reactions to the situation, and the behavior of those around them. In order to manage feelings, it is essential to understand what is causing them and why, and then understand how you feel about it. By remaining aware, resilient people can maintain their control of the situation and think of new ways to tackle problems. Now, much of everything in life is really out of our control, if we want to be very honest with ourselves. But, you can manage and influence situations to minimize the negative impact or to maximize positive outcomes, but you may not be able to control the situation.

6. **Pray and Meditate**

   Praying is when you are talking to God, while meditating is a chance for God to get a word in with you. Find at least 15 minutes a day to be in quietness. At first you may struggle to be still for five minutes but with practice you'll appreciate an hour. This can happen each morning as you face your day or at the end of the day to reflect. What I have come to learn and know is that God does things (1) with me, (2) through me and (3) for me, and each are for my highest and greatest good. I'll elaborate on that a little later as well. But, seek understanding for these storms, i.e. difficulties, to understand why it has happened and what to do next. Understanding will help you to minimize the reoccurrence of the same problems. When you can understand the situation, yourself and/or others, you will see behaviors or patterns to prepare for the next storm. I have always been a woman of faith and I find that being on my knees to praise and weep has served me well. This may sound "religious" but it's far from religion but rather spirituality and mindfulness. So, I use the word prayer and meditation because many people understand these acts. But, call it whatever will help you get up when you fall down. In fact, when I fall down that is when it is easiest to get on my knees since I'm already down there. Pray to share with whatever is your source of strength or whatever you see as greater than yourself. Meditate to listen for comforting and affirming words that speak to your spirit for inner strength.

7. **Don't Be Afraid**

   Fear is nothing to be ashamed of. You will encounter situations in life and in your career which are scary. It can be the loss of a job or better yet, getting a new job. Essentially, being resilient means encountering change and change is difficult. I've been fearful off and on over the last four years. But, for each fear, I identified the cause and conquered it to move on. You can be fearful too long. For years, I stayed in a dysfunctional marriage out of fear. Some people stay in or on a job out of fear, accept a project that doesn't align with their skills or values, and, in short, either fear success or fear failure. You have to release yourself from fear which will allow you to move through the storm.

   Ask yourself, what is holding you back? Is it your thoughts, is it someone, is it fears, etc.? I was fearful of being alone and not being loved. Well, hell I was already in a marriage where I wasn't loved, and I was alone even when he was around. So, that fear was causing me to be miserable. Now the beauty of fear is that we would not have courage, if we did not have fear. Releasing myself from my fear led to the courage to get a divorce. So, identify and face your fear(s). What can you face by summoning up courage that will allow you to live a more authentic life, pursue your passion, etc.? Think of a ship in a storm. The fear of dying will compel the men to do whatever is needed to keep control of the ship that is being tossed about on the waves. But, if they let their fears control them, they may cower in a corner and do nothing, which may lead to certain death. Let fear fuel you: not stop you.

   Lastly, I believe that there are two types of fears: the fear of success and the fear of failure. Fear of success will allow you to take risks, but as you succeed you will often sabotage yourself, while the fear of failure makes it difficult to even take risks because you don't want to ever fail. Both of these can be detrimental to your journey. Figure out which fear is lurking about in order to move forward. Remember resilience is not about a lack of failure. You may fail but then you move on, which is the true meaning of resilience.

8. **Let Your Setback Be a Come Back**

   When you are used to rising, rising and rising like a car on a roller coaster ride, you forget that you have to drop at some point. A professional speaker named Willie Jolly said, "A setback is a setup for a comeback." Your ability to be at ease and resilient are totally dependent upon how you view your storm. No one is inoculated from feeling the stings, pains and worries associated with a storm, but the longer you dwell on the difficulties, the longer you will experience it. See it for what it is, embrace it and move through it. Often a storm can be wind blowing you towards your true passion and purpose: new shores.

9. **Ask for Help**

There is no shame in seeking professional help from people who are trained to help you weather the storm, i.e. psychiatrist, therapist, etc. When you start to feel overwhelmed by what you are experiencing, seek support. I'm glad that I had the wherewithal to know that I needed help when I began to mentally unravel. Unfortunately, those of us who are seen as strong will go at it alone, believing that we have to keep up the appearance of strength. There is more strength in asking for help than suffering in silence. I must emphasize that this is not the same as having a coach, mentor or advocate. You need someone who has a mental wellness background to help you explore your thoughts and feelings, and even look at life circumstances that may be rooted in childhood memories, etc. Even though Vince Lombardi was one of America's greatest football coaches, I wouldn't want him to provide insight about what I just went through. One of his famous quotes was "Winners never quit, and quitters never win." He would have been great for showing me how to improve on motivating employees, which is what a good coach can do. But, he couldn't help me dig deep to put my life's pieces together to make sense of my storms. People make the mistake of tapping into the wrong resource for the wrong reason. Seek a mental wellness professional if you start to feel depressed, have suicidal ideation, lack energy or demonstrate any host of other ailments that are signs of mental distress or rather dis-ease. A coach, a friend, pastor, etc. are great resources but if they do not have a background in mental health, you may be overlooking a significant step to healing from trauma or stress. I was talking with my brother and said that when all this is over I'm going to need a therapist. He agreed and added that I probably have Post Traumatic Stress Disorder (PTSD) to contend with and to sort through. Trust me when I say that certain things, no, I mean many things, in life can cause mental dis-ease.

10. **Being Still**

You may feel that you have to roll up your sleeves and do something. Or, when you feel helpless, you start doing some things to feel as if you are doing something. But, sometimes doing nothing is doing something. Occasionally, you may have to wait out the storm. I have a habit of needing to fix things and constantly doing things. At one point, I was more of a human doing than a human being. Sometimes, we need to let things be so that we can see what is real and what is a FEAR: False Expectations Appearing Real. I hate clichés but sometimes it only makes sense to say them. Some things will work themselves out while others will not, so you must know the difference. Be careful of wanting to do something to the extent that you or it may actually get in the way. The British are known for their resiliency: keep calm and carry on. Learn to be still and let things be. This requires discernment.

11. Maintain Strong Social Connections

Whenever you're dealing with a problem, it is important to have people who can offer support. Talking about the challenges you are facing can be an excellent way to gain perspective, look for new solutions, or simply express your emotions. Friends, family members, co-workers, and online support groups can all be potential sources of social connectivity. But, if you find that people are not willing to support you…don't try to force them into giving you something that they are unwilling or unable to give. Be selective about sharing your situation. It should be with people who are worthy of your stuff. I have learned that my plight is heavy and takes another strong person to shoulder the weight. More importantly, understand that you cannot maintain healthy connections if you do not have them. So, start by creating those relationships for when you need that support. Don't wait to dig your well when you are thirsty.

Someone once shared with me that we can't create new old friends. There is some truth to that. What we need during a storm are people who get us, understand our pain, have the background information for context and maybe have been through a few storms with us before. I can share this with new, great friends but they didn't know 'me' before all this occurred, so they cannot truly empathize with what I actually lost. They can only listen and show compassion based on their frame of reference. They don't remember when I started my business with nothing but a rolodex (most people won't even know what that is) working in an unfinished basement with the pink insulation showing. I literally scrapped and climbed my way to the top. Or, as those who have known me before I started the business can attest, when I stood in food lines to care for my infant son. People who have walked along side of you can offer you a far greater type of support. New people have only heard about my nice office space, 100 employees and the many awards and accolades. They cannot imagine the magnitude of my loss. But, those who have been alongside of me understand and can give a different level of empathy, compassion and pep talk that new acquaintances or friends are unable to give. I said all that to say that you should work on building new relationships and nurture existing relationships.

12. Identify as a Survivor, Not as a Victim

When dealing with any potential crisis, it is essential to view yourself as a survivor. Avoid thinking like a victim of that circumstance and instead look for ways to resolve the problem. You may have been victimized, but you don't have to remain a victim when you can be a victor. If you continue to tell yourself that you are a victim, you will begin to behave and believe that you are a victim which brings its own set of limitations.

Feed new information into your subconscious. Create a theme song for yourself…such as *I Will Survive* or the *Rocky Theme Song*. I have selected a few songs that I play over and over in my head as a reminder of my ability to weather the storm and be victorious regardless of the outcome. I also have a playlist that includes songs with inspiring lyrics that I may play while getting dressed in the morning or throughout the day.

13. Don't Fight It, but Move with It

The storm will often take you to far away shores that you may have never considered. In moving with the storm, you may discover new skills that can assist you in navigating that storm. I love a song titled "The Greatest," by Kenny Rogers about a boy's discovery of his strengths. The story goes a little like this: there was a little boy who grabbed his ball, hat and bat and left to go play baseball alone. He would say to himself, "…I am the greatest player of them all…" He would throw the ball up, swing, and the ball would hit the ground. He missed - it was a strike. Again, he threw the ball up, swung and the ball hit the ground. He did this for hours as he looked into the pretend crowd, hearing the fans cheer his name. He never lost confidence that he was the best baseball hitter ever, as he threw the ball up, swung and the ball hit the ground. Now, it's getting late and he hadn't hit the ball, but he hasn't given up either. Before heading home for the day, he shouted, "I am the greatest that is a fact," as he dug into the dirt with his feet, threw the ball up in the air and swung with all his might; still the ball hit the ground. He picked up the ball and said, "I am the greatest that is understood, but even I didn't know I could pitch that good." Don't give up; keep swinging your bat during times of difficulties and you may discover new skills, a new purpose or even a new direction to go during your storm. That's what being resilient is all about.

Move with the flow, as the song goes, 'row, row, row your boat, gently down the stream…" You aren't a salmon trying to go up the stream for mating. So, allow yourself to move into new areas and territories based on where the current and/or wind is taking you. Just maybe that is the direction you should have been headed but you needed other influences to get your attention. Maybe like the boy, you are better at something else, but you keep trying to be what you are expected to be or have told yourself to be and that is creating the storm.

Anyone of my storms, individually, could have been debilitating. I could have thrown in the towel and decided to quit or simply given up. Each storm wreaked havoc for me mentally, physically and financially, especially, financially. No. To be honest, it was an equal share of destruction and devastation, mentally, physically, financially, and let's add spiritually. Each impacted one another. But, my perfect storm carried an imperfect person to Asia. It was the best thing that could have ever happened to me. Yes, I lost everything that I thought was of value, but I found me. I found people who embraced me. I improved and deepened my relationships with my sons; and I gained an incredible love for life and people. The list of what I've gained through my loss is inexhaustible. Where I was rich in material wealth, I am now richer on so many other levels. I believe that I was blessed with a horrific but 'perfect' storm, just for me. When you are encountering storms, try some if not all of these suggestions to help you along the way. For now, continue to read through this book and pay close attention to the next chapter about forgiveness. That was a game changer for me. I will end this chapter with one of my ultimate, favorite quote:

> "And once the storm is over you won't remember how you made it through, how you managed to survive. You won't even be sure, in fact, whether the storm is really over. But one thing is certain. When you come out of the storm you won't be the same person who walked in. That's what this storm's all about."

Haruki Murakami

Chapter 4

Forgiveness and Letting Go: A Game Changer

In life, on the job and your career, you will encounter people who will hurt you in many ways. You may be betrayed, abandoned, harassed, lied to, lied on, falsely accused, physically abused, mentally abused, financially abused, used, or cheated on; and the list goes on. Unfortunately, all of these may be done by family and friends. Some things we can forgive and let go of fairly quickly because family or friends are involved, while some things we will carry with us because it is family or friends. Even in the carrying of issues with us, we may choose to continue the relationship, or we may become estranged from family or end a friendship. However, when it comes to family you had no choice in who was able to be in your life. You didn't choose your siblings, parents, extended family and so on. So, some things you had to put up with and make an effort to get past, for the sake of the family.

But, hurtful acts don't just stop with family; these things happen with coworkers, colleagues and even clients. In all fairness, you chose the people you work with by nature of maintaining employment somewhere, especially if you are a manager or leader. In all cases, you chose the job or the company. So, what do you do when the choices you have made cause distress? Or, rather what do you do when it is coworkers, colleagues, companies, clients, etc. who have wronged you in some way? It seems much harder to reconcile in our hearts and minds how to forgive and get over things at work. We often don't know how to handle it. Often, we are less inclined to forgive or let go because we don't place the same value or have the same level of investment in our work relationships as we do with family, for the most part. To not forgive or let go will mean losing a significant part of our life, lifestyle, happiness, etc., so we do it for the greater good, with family, right?

What prompted me to write about forgiveness and letting go is that nearly everyone says it to someone at some point or another, and we all need to do it at some point in our lives. Parents tell their children to forgive, friends tell us to let things go and then nearly every religious teaching mentions forgiveness and letting go, but nothing tells us how. There's no instructional guide or handbook to help us to get over stuff. This became a quest for me during my perfect storm. I wanted to know about it for personal growth and usage. I looked everywhere and would ask people, "How?" Everyone kept saying "Just let it go." But, when I asked how to forgive and let it go, they would repeat themselves. You can't explain a phenomenon with the same words. You can't just say 'let it go' as if it were bungee jumping and all you have to do is jump. I needed someone to tell me how because I wanted to forgive and let go of some of the pain that nearly killed me. And, I wanted to know how to do this for the minor incidents that kept me awake at night. What about you? Wouldn't you get a better night's sleep if you could let some things go? I wanted to know what the process was, what letting go would feel like or how I would know when I actually forgave or let go. I had more questions than answers.

I find that because our career is such a significant part of our life, it is important to be able to forgive and let go in that arena for peace of mind and ongoing success. I have, personally and professionally, discovered that not letting go can create obstacles, both seen and unseen. It's easy to forgive small infractions but when there are life-altering incidents, it can be an overwhelming proposition to forgive and/or let go. For instance, take siblings who engage in the occasional bickering; they get mad with one another and then make up. However, one day one of the sisters does something so heinous that the other sister wants to exact revenge, but their mom says that the hurt sister needs to forgive her sister. What does that mean? Does it mean that she should be okay with what her sister has done? No. Does it mean that the mom will punish the other sister? Maybe. Does it mean she should continue doing sister type things until her sibling does something else? I dunno. Does it mean the sister shouldn't feel slighted? Hmmm. What does it mean? Parents don't tell us 'how' to forgive; they tell us to forgive with no instructions. We never learn the art of forgiveness or the process. As adults, we are just as bewildered when terrible things happen, and we stumble through life asking more and more questions without getting the answers that we need to move on.

I want you to stop and think about a time someone did something egregious at work that you considered to be a wrongful act towards you. What were the circumstances and how did you feel? Depending on whether you have forgiven them or not, you probably don't like the way it feels to remember what that person or group did. And, this is all dependent on whether or not you got closure. Would it have helped if someone apologized? Maybe or maybe not. So, what did you need to forgive? Or rather, what do you need if you haven't forgiven that person or group? Sometimes time will heal, but is that forgiveness, letting go or just forgetting? Then there are times when time doesn't help; especially if it negatively impacted your career or altered your life.

I believe it is important to talk about forgiveness in the work place. So much happens on a day-to-day basis and sometimes no one stops to see if everyone is okay. Yet we continue moving on until we reach a breaking point where enough is enough and then it's difficult to let go of all the stuff we have stored up. In the workplace we need to practice forgiveness and letting go to move on with the peace that forgiveness brings. That is what this chapter is about. It's a game changer.

I used to share with people that when others threw bricks at me, I would throw them back because I am instinctively a fighter. But, I noticed that I also took some of those bricks and built a wall. That wasn't the answer. Many people shield themselves from possible hurt by putting up a wall. And, lobbing bricks over the wall isn't the answer either. That is basically revenge. But what are we mere mortals to do when people hurl bricks at us? Keep in mind a brick can be an attack, harassment, insult, betrayal, lie, etc. With over 25 years under my belt as a professional, I have seen some mess in both my career and in the careers of others. Crap happens that can destroy you and all that you've worked to achieve, and it can be perplexing to figure out how to forgive when there is someone to blame but no one takes the blame or tries to right the wrong. In short, what do you do with those damn bricks?

I am sure you can think of a time when you were negatively impacted by a colleague. It could have been as minor as being given incorrect data that you presented at a leadership meeting. I say this is minor even though it could have been a huge snafu. It's minor because maybe the person did not do it maliciously. Yes, you were given bad information and maybe you got a black eye from it, but the coworker was genuinely sorry. Or, it could have been when you were told that the promotion was yours for the taking and then your colleague whom you trusted and confided in leaked information that caused your boss to hire an outside candidate even though you were well qualified. You felt betrayed, used and lied to. But, what can you do? Maybe you can relate to being a scientist who has his boss review his paper and then the boss shares his ideas in a meeting as if they were his own.

There are countless ways to feel wronged in the workplace. As mentioned before, you only have three ways to ultimately deal with it: 1.) stay and take it, 2.) stay and change it or 3.) leave. Regardless of what you do, there are under-pinning feelings that can range from embarrassment to rage depending on what happened. And, the worst part is that if you haven't forgiven the transgressor, you will carry with you those feelings and negative thoughts whether you stay and take it, stay and change it or leave. You are going to feel some type of way for hours or even years, depending on what happened and why it happened. Then some people take it to their grave. If you forgive that person and let it go, you can move forward easier and faster.

When you carry with you resentment, anger, hurt, etc., it becomes heavy like chains around your neck or rather your mind, body and soul. We sink into depression, we begin to have physical symptoms that manifest in ways like headaches, ulcers, weight gain/loss, sleeplessness and more. Can you see how this can impact your performance and productivity? I was working with a client on a project; wherein, we needed to select a few employees to be a part of a team for a variety of assignments. This project was a high-profile assignment that would be a nice ticket to have stamped, right? The core team met with me to identify employees to bring on to the project. I met with the initial team as the contractor. As colleagues' names were tossed into the ring, one name was jumped on immediately. Let's just say the name Mary Smith was proposed as a potential team member. Let's say Theresa is one of the existing team members. This is how the dialogue went on that day in that very well-known organization that could boast of having intelligent employees. "I think Mary Smith would be great for the marketing aspect of this project," said one member. Theresa blurts out vehemently, "That bitch...I will not stay on the project if she's on the team." I was shocked at the response and asked her why. Theresa said, "I worked with her nine years ago on an awards program and she sabotaged me." Theresa was still angry. She explained what happened as if it were yesterday. She had carried with her what had happened for all those years - nine to be exact. I believe that when it was happening, she was probably negatively impacted in such a way that it caused great distress. She has neither forgiven or forgotten the incident or the person. The problem with such is that she is still impacted by it. In some ways, she may be even limiting her career success by not having that person on her team. So, the impact of not having forgiveness takes its toll in many ways. Some at the table may have thought that she should let it go but they may not understand the depth of Theresa's pain, what she experienced because of Mary's act, and so forth. But, I do know that she is still affected by Mary because she hasn't forgiven Mary and/or the others involved.

Chapter 4: Forgiveness and Letting Go: A Game Changer

My dear… things happen. Sometimes there are things that we may have caused and then there are things that happen to us by no fault of our own. But, the way through these situations is to forgive and to let it go. It's no small feat to do either. Some refuse to forgive as if this will punish the other person or they hold on to things to include pain as a badge of honor.

So why is forgiveness and letting go relevant to playing the game? I want you to stop for a second and write down the name of someone whom you enjoy spending as much time as possible with. Now, look at that name and think about your coworkers. Unless you work with that person whose name you wrote down, you spend more time with your coworkers than that person. We spend on average 10 to 12 hours with colleagues while with children or significant others we spend on average three to four hours tops since you should not count sleep as spending time together. It is quite simple: we spend more time with people at work than in any other part of our lives. It behooves us to have healthy relationships. And to be quite honest, people are going to make mistakes. Some mistakes will cause you distress, like being terminated because of layoffs when you felt as if your boss could have protected you based on his power and influence; while other mistakes may take little to no time to repair, like not being invited to a coworker's son's wedding when others on the team were invited. Whatever the infraction, at the end of the day, you gotta forgive and even let it go, especially if it is causing distress for you. But what does that look like and how do you do it? That is the question that I have asked of so many people from diverse walks of life, different social status, various religious beliefs, etc. No one has been able to give me a good answer.

Forgiveness prevalence is a religious, legal, and philosophical matter (virtue), and a social science and psychology construct. It is the most elusive act with many theories and meanings. I read an online article by Greater Good Science Center at UC Berkeley that stated, "Psychologists generally define forgiveness as a conscious, deliberate decision to release feelings of resentment or vengeance toward a person or group who has harmed you, regardless of whether they actually deserve your forgiveness." Forgiveness is becoming such a popular notion so much so that – Forgiveness Day is on the first Sunday of August. Wouldn't it be nice to send or receive a forgiveness card? I'm sure that would facilitate the healing process of letting go.

As for letting go, what is that about? So often we hear that phrase that it sounds like a cliché when it is being said to you. It is just as difficult as forgiving. Letting go is when you give up believing that you can change the past. The act of letting go is to stop holding on to something whether it is an actual entity, thought or belief. I like to verify and validate things especially after my journey of working on a Ph.D. It is a natural inclination for me to want to know the real definition or what others have said about certain things. I first looked it up on Webster which didn't recognize the words, at least not both words together, i.e. letting go. I started reading through many definitions, articles and even the Urban Dictionary. Everyone was saying pretty much the same thing that I said. Cambridge Dictionary defines letting go as "To stop thinking about or being angry about the past or something that happened in the past." None of these truly suffice for me but they are a good start. I think that letting go is very subjective and only you can determine the true definition. But, if you are really struggling with letting go, I suggest that you do some additional reading, aside from what I'm about to share with you.

Here's a message to those who are thinking that they know someone who needs to let something go: I would highly suggest that you don't go to them and stick this book in their face and say, "See, you need to let it go." Nothing is more irritating than having people tell you to let something go when they have no earthly idea how something has impacted you mentally, physically and/or spiritually (which is also considered emotions). To add insult to injury, they can't tell you how to let it go! So, if you really want to be a friend or supporter, listen and provide some insight to help them understand that they need to let something go. You cannot force anyone into letting go; it has to happen in their own time. And, they must believe that such is in their best interest.

Forgiveness and letting go are not one and the same. If I don't get anything else out on paper, I want to make sure that this is understood. Forgiveness and letting go are not synonymous; however, if you use each as a tool you will experience a greater level of success. It takes strength to do both separately and when you accomplish both you will be able to move on from any circumstance that has created obstacles or a roadblock, either physically, mentally or emotionally.

I've shared with audiences bits and pieces of my professional journey which have become my personal story during speaking engagements on the topic of resilience. I never seem to tell the whole story because it's so intricate and complicated, with too many variances, twists and turns. Although, to say someone embezzled from my company and left me in dire straits is easy to understand. But, there are so many other facets that I haven't mentioned because what has been kept in the dark is continuing to surface from the criminal investigation. Whenever I speak about my own personal and professional storms and how to be resilient to weather your own storms, the feedback that I get is amazing. But get this: the question that is top of mind for many people is whether I've forgiven the people who have caused some of my heartaches, tribulations and significant losses in my career, and ultimately my life. I say my life because I was one with my career, until recently.

Allow me to digress a little here. I loved what I did so much that I allowed my success, business and work to become my identity. That is very natural in a society that values success and accomplishments. Is it right or wrong? Only you can answer that for yourself. It was right for me because I lived through my business, which was my career. You will notice that at any social function when people are introduced, the conversation will go a little like this: "Hello, my name is Austin." "Hey, Austin, nice to meet you. My name is Chad. What do you do?" "I work for xyz. I'm a Financial Planner. What about you? What do you do?" I cannot recall a time when that wasn't how the conversation started. Oh, except in settings where people are there for spirituality/religion. Then people will lead with "What church do you attend?" or if it's a function for your kids, then they will lead with either "Which one is yours?" (referring to your child to make sure you aren't some weirdo just there to prey on the little ones) or "What school do your kids attend?" And, then the conversation leads into the work questions. So, there are exceptions, but generally where you work or what you do helps people to know you. All of the questions are basically small talk and qualifiers to some extent but that's another subject. The point is that many people wrap who they are into their job, title, position and even company. I did, and it worked for me. I now wrap my identity in what I do or rather how I contribute to society. But, if that should for some reason stop adding value or start to be a burden for me, I would be challenged to let it go, too.

In working with a variety of clients in leadership positions, I'm often privy to conversations that are behind closed doors. I've worked with many of my clients for well over ten years, and I have heard some back-office conversations from people who carry a grudge or resentment towards coworkers for deeds that happened long ago. It seems that forgiveness in the workplace is not discussed nor practiced to a healthy extent, and that can make for an arduous existence at a workplace or within a career.

I felt compelled to include this chapter in the book based on my journey. I am writing another book about this journey and other life-altering situations, but I wanted to give you a back drop on why forgiveness and letting go are important and that, if I can, I believe that you can too regardless of your situation. I shared information about the perfect storm because I had to forgive my wasband for what felt like extortion. It was less about the money and more about how he did what he did and all that he took from me when we were friends. I had to forgive my ex-employee because thoughts of her while researching the embezzlement and living a nightmare for several years took me to a very dark place. And, I had to forgive God for what I felt was abandonment which I'll discuss later, yeah. Then I had to forgive myself which was the most difficult to achieve.

I don't know if I would have written about forgiveness or letting go when I was in my 20s, 30s or even 40s. I'm not even sure it is about age, time or circumstances. But, over time and having experienced things in life that I could not have imagined when I was younger, I have learned that things are so much easier when you can forgive, and let's not even talk about letting go yet. Let's take baby steps, yeah. So, for me, I attribute some of this to age and career maturity coupled with other things that I'll discuss in later chapters. I hope by now you recognize that forgiveness is important. In the workplace, here are reasons why it is important:

- It frees you up to collaborate and foster healthy relationships;
- Communications shut down without it;
- It impacts performance and productivity;
- People self-isolate, i.e. physically and/or mentally, you separate from the people involved or the situation/environment;
- It festers and sometimes infects not just you but the entire workplace, in general;
- People become nonresponsive; and,
- Unconscious sabotage happens.

Forgiveness

You would think that I would deal with this subject in the Resilience or Spirituality chapters, right? I may have touched upon it; however, forgiveness is merely one individual spoke in the wheel of career management. The spokes that we typically think of are performance, communications, business acumen, management, etc. a balanced combination of knowledge, skills and abilities to strengthen the wheel. But, we often don't consider forgiveness as a necessary spoke. However, if you visualize yourself riding a bicycle, and the wheel is missing one or two spokes, I can assure you that within time you are going to get a flat if you hit a pot hole or, at a minimum, a wobbly ride where it is difficult to steer in a straight path. You need the spoke that represents forgiveness.

Chapter 4: Forgiveness and Letting Go: A Game Changer

As I mentioned earlier, we readily forgive friends and family. But, I think that professional forgiveness is more noble and difficult. You see, it is easier to give up on people at work because we believe they don't matter or that we don't have to live with them. As I pointed out, we spend more time with coworkers than anyone else in our life, so career maturity is demonstrated when we are able to forgive colleagues, clients and competitors.

When you have been wronged, over time you begin to resent the act, the person involved and maybe yourself for not doing something that made you feel whole again. "Resentment is like taking poison and waiting for the other person to die," said Malachy McCourt. That quote can be applied to not forgiving in general. When forgiveness is absent, then resentment sets in. We often hold on to grudges, resentment and anger as if we are hurting the other person. Forgiveness is occasionally given in personal relationships but seldom practiced in the workplace and often not in our professional life, which is why pages are flying off physicians' prescription pads to provide us with sleep aids, antidepressants, antacids, ulcer medicines, pain relievers, etc. Hmm, a dose of forgiveness may be all you need! As an HR practitioner, I can tell you that what comes along with the inability to forgive costs an organization a lot of time and money from workflow stoppage to sick days taken. When you forgive, that does not mean you gloss over or deny the seriousness of an offense against you. It does not mean forgetting, nor does it condone or excuse the offense. To let go of anger or a debilitating feeling that prevents you from being whole or happy grants you freedom. It is not about the other person; it's about your well-being. It is to recognize the pain you suffered without letting the pain define you; thus, enabling you to heal and move on.

Forgiveness and letting go can cause or rather allow you to be happy while improving your health, and it frees you from a cell with no walls. But, that is easier said than done, right?

I attribute my near-death experiences to the pain that I felt from betrayal; the hate directed at Tammy was consuming me. I resented her for her betrayal, theft and negatively altering my life. And, you just read what resentment meant. If I did not let it go, I think I would not be here today. In truth, if I didn't forgive, I don't think that I could have written this book. I was becoming crippled in mind, body and spirit. I now have a life where the flow of goodness is no longer blocked. I'm healing from the inside out, and I'm happy again. I'm even smiling right now because I know that all is well and right with my soul.

Forgiveness and letting go, huh? As I mentioned, no one tells us how, but enough people tell us that we should, which should indicate that it is the right thing to do. What I can do is share with you how I did it, and give you techniques that you can incorporate and practice:

1. **See Forgiveness as Gift for You and Not as a Reward for Someone Else**

    Don't get bogged down in believing that if you forgive someone, then he gets away with something that he did wrong. No one ever truly gets away with anything; I assure you. But to not forgive is punishing yourself. The offenders don't feel it unless they have to interact with you regularly and you constantly remind them of their deed and how it impacted you. But, even that will cause you more distress than them if they ignore you; or even deny that what you are feeling, thinking or believing can be attributed to them; or if they deflect it as if it is in your head, not accurate or even false. Being angry, upset and resentful towards someone doesn't lighten your load; it holds you down. So, forgiveness is for you to lift the heaviness that someone else caused.

2. **Replace Anger with Compassion - Try to Understand Why They Did What They Did**

    There is sometimes justification for what people do (at least in their mind), and then there is never justification for what some people do. Don't try to make up reasons for the person so that you can feel better; but do try to understand why they did something from their vantage point and apply compassion. I asked my wasband why he was basically taking all my money. He said that he had to look out for himself. He didn't say anything about the kids, just himself. He couldn't care less about my well-being. Well, I can look back and see that my wasband grew up in poverty and had always had a fear and issue with being poor. He took from me to satisfy his own insecurities around money. That is not justification, but I understand. I have moments when I feel some sadness for him because with all that I have lost I am not afraid of being 'poor'. That was his issue! He may still be struggling with that because what he was dealing with was internal: perceivably there will never be enough. How very sad for him. You need to attempt to see that it is less about you and more about them. Hurt people hurt people. Try to see why they hurt and you may discover why they are hurting. This means looking at a situation causing distress so that you can empathize with the transgressor about their transgression.

Say for instance, you are friends with a colleague in the finance department. A budget is eliminated that included your pet project that you worked hard on for years and lobbied to launch on the international stage. You are given the option to go to another role with less pay or to resign, i.e. leave. This came as a blindside (a blindside is a football term that means to not see a hit coming). You are thinking, what the heck, and you believe that your supposed friend should have told you because that budget cut had been discussed for months within his department. It is the first of the year and you have spent money during the holidays that you would have otherwise saved, if only you knew of the impending cut that significantly impacted your personal budget, too. You feel betrayed by your friend. But, sit in his seat for a moment. That supposed friend may have been more of a friend than you can imagine. Maybe there is a policy that prohibits him from discussing budget cuts, etc., because it is a part of an impending merger. Maybe there are some issues with lawsuits that caused him to have to sit on the information. But, what you also don't know is that he fought for you in that room, he was torn up over this, and now he lost a friend because you are angry with him. Compassion can help you to ease your pain, not someone else's pain; unless you show them that compassion. As Wayne Dyer said, "When we change the way we see things, the things we see will change." See someone differently and maybe you'll see the situation differently; thus, allowing you to forgive.

3. **Replace the Hurt with Energy Directed Elsewhere**

The emotions we feel when we feel wronged consume a lot of energy, so much so that we sometimes gotta take a nap. It's tiring! Channel that energy into something else and somewhere else for your greater good. Turn that negative energy into positive energy. Here's something crazy. When you get twisted and want to strike out because you are so mad, hurt or whatever, give someone a hug. Energy is energy, whether positive or negative. You could be sitting at your desk and someone who has done something to you walks by and you immediately see red and start obsessing over how you want to exact revenge. Sometimes, you can be so angry that you literally feel as if you will explode. At that moment, exert that energy by channeling it into something beneficial for yourself, like going to the gym, cleaning your office, climbing the stair well while reciting positive affirmations, etc. Can you imagine what it would be like if we were able to bottle energy? Use that energy to take care of chores around the house or to volunteer somewhere. Hey, it's about choices. What are you going to do with that negativity so that you are whole, again? That negative energy can be fuel to ignite your passion or power something positive.

4. **Make a Conscious Decision to Feel Better and Heal**

   Now, you can't make this up. A guy friend was angry about his ex-wife to the point he was miserable. He asked me how was it that I was happy after all the misfortune and absurdity that I had gone through, and in a sense, am still going through. I told him that I have forgiven people. I suggested that he do the same. With all the seriousness he had left in him, he said, that he'll have to be unhappy because he could never forgive his ex-wife. And, he is still unhappy and wounded. It's a conscious decision to be such. I even played a song titled "Intro," by J. Cole. The song is set to a beautiful melody, but the words are simplistic. The lyrics repetitively says, "Do you wanna be, happy. Do you wanna, do you wanna be, happy?" This guy wasn't budging; he held on to that pain like it was a badge he earned in the Boys Scouts of America. If he could be honest with himself, he'll discover that his unwillingness to feel better is feeding something inside. Maybe his pain is better than feeling nothing, which is problematic. In some sense, he has something to hold on to, which some people will choose as a viable option.

5. **Put Things in Perspective and Acknowledge Your Own Inner Pain and Why**

   You may have to step back and figure out why what happened to you hurts so much. So, you didn't get selected to be in a program that would give you an inside track for a promotion. There will be other programs, but your boss promised you that you were in line for that slot. To make matters worse, the slot was given to someone whom you believe didn't deserve it. What is really going on? Is it the program, your boss's decision to do something else, or jealousy towards the person who got what you wanted? Could it be that you feel like the kid on the playground who wasn't selected to be on the team? Are there some unresolved issues that you have with rejection or authority figures who have let you down before? Sometimes we can make something so personal that we lose sight that what happened is insignificant to what we are feeling, based on past scars of which we are unaware. Spend time looking at the entire situation to determine what exactly causes the resentment, hurt or pain. Then be honest with yourself on why it is impacting you so that you can deal with the real issue. Sometimes hurt can be misdirected.

6. **Humanize the Other Person**

   There is a movie titled *Midnight Clear* that I watched many years ago and loved. It's about humanizing the enemy. Here is a description of the movie I pulled from the Internet:

Chapter 4: Forgiveness and Letting Go: A Game Changer

In the early phase of the Battle of the Bulge in December 1944, a small US Army intelligence and reconnaissance squad is sent to occupy a deserted chateau near the German lines to gather information on the enemy's movements. Losses from an earlier patrol have reduced the squad to just six men: Sgt. Knott, Miller, Avakian, Shutzer, Wilkins and Mundy. On their way to the chateau, they discover the frozen corpses of a German and an American in a standing embrace, seemingly arranged by the Germans as a grim joke. Settling into their temporary home, they soon discover they are not alone. A group of German soldiers have occupied a position nearby. While out on patrol, Knott, Mundy and Shutzer see a trio of German soldiers aiming their weapons at them, but the enemy then vanish without shooting. The Germans, clearly more skilled and experienced than the young GIs, soon leave calling cards, start a snowball fight one evening and offer a Christmas truce. At first, the Americans think the Germans are taunting them, but it eventually becomes clear that the enemy wants to parlay.

A second film based on a true story is Joyeux Noel. It is about a group of soldiers in World War I that agree to an unofficial truce, which begins when the Scots begin to sing festive songs from home, accompanied by bagpipes. Here is an overview pulled from Wikipedia:

Sprink and Sørensen arrive in the German front-line and Sprink sings for his comrades. As Sprink sings "Silent Night" he is accompanied by a piper in the Scottish front-line. Sprink responds to the piper and exits his trench with a small Christmas tree singing "Adeste Fideles". Following Sprink's lead, the French, German and Scottish officers meet in no-man's-land and agree on a cease-fire for the evening. The various soldiers met and wished each other "Joyeux Noël," "Frohe Weihnachten", and "Merry Christmas." They exchange chocolate, champagne and photographs of loved ones. Horstmayer gives Audebert back his wallet, with a photograph of his wife inside, lost in the attack a few days prior, and they connect over pre-war memories. Palmer and the Scots celebrate a brief Mass for the soldiers (in Latin as was the practice in the Catholic Church at that time) and the soldiers retire deeply moved.

I share these two movies because it demonstrates what can be achieved when we humanize the enemy. When we chose to forgive, we cannot see the other person as the monster that they typically become in our mind. We must see them as people who make mistakes. Just recently, I was watching a movie and one of the characters looked like what I imagined my ex-employee, Tammy, would look like as a little girl. I smiled and asked myself, "I wonder how she is doing?" It was as if I had forgotten what she had done for a moment. That felt good. I believe that she needs to go to jail for her crime, but she is no monster that should be executed, which is what I wanted for the first two years of dealing with my losses after her betrayal and embezzlement. I no longer seek revenge but rather justice.

7. Express Those Emotions in Non-hurtful Ways

One of the most important things you can do is to let the person know that they have harmed you or how you feel if you are able to speak directly with the person. If you are unable to talk with him or her, then write a letter. Sometimes people may not even know that they hurt or harmed you. They may know that what they did was wrong, but maybe they don't know how it has impacted you. You owe it to yourself and them to get things right.

8. Tell the Story as Long as You Need to; It's a Process

Now, this is totally about me. This is something that I have to do to move through the forgiveness phase. I tell everyone what happened (sometimes to the point I wear out whomever I regard as a confidant) and I write about it in my journal. I keep telling the same story and what I notice is that when I finally stop talking about it, I've pretty much purged. There is no way that I could keep it all bottled up inside. I need to talk about it with people whom I trust and respect. Earlier I said that I keep my issues to myself. That is true: I don't tell everyone everything. So, I share my story within my inner circle. But, I do this for another reason as well. I, also, want other peoples' perspectives. Maybe it's me; maybe I overreacted or something, or maybe I have a blind spot preventing me from seeing the situation clearly. So, I get other people's opinion(s). This works for me, but I caution you that if it is someone at work, be mindful that telling your story may place the other person in a bad light or even cause more problems for you. This is when you need to tap into your Support based on the C.A.R.S. concept that I wrote about in the second book.

Be mindful that retelling the same story may drive people away, so understand that everyone is not going to see or feel the same way about your situation. If it becomes too heavy, I recommend that you see a therapist. I was on a business trip and this man I was sitting beside in business class shared with me that every successful business owner needs a good tax attorney and a good therapist. He said that the tax attorney will protect my money while the therapist will protect my mind. Figure out who you can and need to speak with to process what is going on in your head.

9. **Give Up on Expecting to Change the Past**

Realizing you cannot change the past is what letting go is about, and forgiveness makes it a lot easier. As we know, the definition of insanity is doing the same thing over and over and expecting different results. The road to anguish is to expect the past to change. *Music of the Heart* is another movie that brings home the message of forgiveness. It is a true story about a violin teacher named Roberta Guaspari who created a high school music program more or less out of thin air in East Harlem, and eventually found herself and her students on the stage at Carnegie Hall. The story is about Roberta's difficult story of struggle and triumph, played by Meryl Streep. It all started with her struggling to make ends meet after her husband left her. His leaving turned her world inside out and she couldn't change that situation. But, she moved on; thus, she let go. Towards the end, she had finally achieved success. There is a scene where she is getting ready for her students' big debut at Carnegie Hall. A limousine arrives, and Roberta rips a button off her beautiful gown. What a disaster! But, her mother who is her supporter brings out a sewing kit and starts sewing the gown. Roberta and her mother are in the limousine, and the mother while repairing Roberta's dress casually says without even looking up, "If Dave hadn't left and divorced you, you would still be at home. If you were still at home, you would not be teaching those students. If you weren't teaching those students, you wouldn't be having this concert. If you weren't having this concert you wouldn't be wearing this gown. If you weren't wearing this gown with a button that needed sewing, I wouldn't be here, sitting here sewing the button back on. You see, you should thank Dave." I loved it! What perspective. By the way, my wasband's name is Dave.

This may be a good time to add that my wasband Dave is, in fact, a good man and a good father. We are rebuilding our friendship and bond, and I can't change what happened during the divorce, but I forgive him, and I hope that he'll forgive me for whatever role I may have played in the deterioration of our friendship.

10. Recognize Your Role in the Deed and Forgive Yourself for Whatever Role You May have Played

There may be instances where you were completely the victim. You did absolutely nothing. I don't believe we have to say that something bad happened to someone because of them. Sometimes bad things happen to good people because of bad people. So, you don't have to blame yourself for everything or anything sometimes. Some people do things to us that we don't deserve. But, we sometimes contribute to a situation as well. Maybe you consistently or sporadically (which is worse) don't turn things in on time and you create a reputation for yourself of being unreliable. Now, I say sporadically is worse. At least consistency allows me to know what to expect. So, say you don't always get projects in to your boss or team on time. Something comes up that is very important, and you are not asked to be on the team or someone does your work and submits it. Yes, you have the right to be mad and you should speak with whomever did it to have closure and an understanding going forward. But, you have to own up to the fact that you are not dependable. You contributed to the situation.

Take my embezzlement case. I did not deserve what happened by any stretch of the imagination. But a lesson learned is that I need to have a better understanding of financials if I am going to continue owning and operating a business. It was my responsibility to have an audit, to have lines of separation and so forth. I allowed her way too much autonomy and I trusted her completely. Now, her unethical behavior and theft are her character flaws that I did not know about or shouldn't be responsible for, but I can learn from this by exploring what role I played. Some things are merely a lesson we must learn, so that we don't continue to make the same mistakes. The things she did are in line with things a con artist will do to betray or fool you. I was completely the victim, but not without taking some ownership. Ownership doesn't mean being at fault.

11. Give Yourself Permission to Grieve and Move Through Your Feelings Knowing that It Takes Time

I speak about the Kübler-Ross Model on Death and Dying Cycle when I coach on change. A Swiss psychiatrist, Kübler-Ross, first introduced her five-stage grief model in her book *On Death and Dying*. Kübler-Ross' model was based on her work with terminally ill patients and has received much criticism in the years since. Mainly because people studying her model mistakenly believed this is the specific order in which people grieve and that all people go through all stages. Kübler-Ross now notes that these stages are not linear, and some people may not experience any of them. Yet and still, others might only undergo two stages rather than all five, one stage, or three stages, etc. It is now more readily known that these five stages of grief are the most commonly-observed experiences by the grieving population.

Also, I have incorporated the Death and Dying Cycle into my change management programs because change means leaving something behind: the death of something. Any loss can cause you to feel as if you are going through the cycle. A break up, termination, quitting and leaving friends behind, loss in pay, etc. can be attributed to these stages that people move through. I recommend that you explore all these stages to understand what you are feeling and thinking: Denial, Anger, Bargaining, Depression and Acceptance.

The wheels started turning when my wasband Dave, who was Tammy's boss, was able to get into the computer that held my company's accounting system that Tammy managed. He discovered her deceit. When I discovered that Tammy was stealing from me, initially it was assumed to be $100,000. I didn't believe it and requested an audit. I actually said, "Well, she deserved it after the many years of being a loyal and faithful confidant." I was disappointed, but not angry: I was in denial. Two different CPAs worked on the files and kept reporting things back to me. I couldn't believe it. It wasn't until it exceeded half a million dollars that I became enraged; thus, I moved into anger. I wanted to hire a hitman to abduct her and do some horrible things to her, but not kill her. I wanted her to live disfigured and so forth. I will spare you the dark details because I'm no longer there, but I'm sure, you get the point.

Then, I became depressed. Depression can cause you to be someone whom you aren't and think even darker thoughts than what anger causes. That is when I wanted her to be tortured and killed. I was consumed with revenge! As I started losing everything because of her embezzlement (I owed several companies while she pocketed the money, and allegedly stole my identity to get credit cards), hopelessness started to set in, which is a part of depression. That's when I started contemplating murder-suicide. My world was shattered, and I couldn't bear another day of the harassment, loss, shame, etc. I knew exactly who was the source of my despair. So, I created a mental list and shared with my support group that if I am missing from a meeting one week, just turn on the news and you'll probably see where I started at one end of the city and made my way across town killing people on a murder suicide list. This caused grave concern, so I said that I was joking, as everyone looked at each other, at me and then the counselor in utter shock. I stopped attending my group therapy because by law the counselor was supposed to report such threats and I wasn't sure whether I would say that again or something worse. I didn't want anyone showing up at my door with handcuffs or a strait-jacket, adding to my current problems. I tell you what; I was a hot ass mess.

Then death showed up at my doorstep and sat next to me on my hospital bed. That is when I started bargaining. The point is, those few years took me on a horrible roller coaster ride. There must have been an electrical wire short in the ride because it wouldn't stop. I kept going around and around with those horrible drops and turns. But, then one day, going into the fourth year, I moved into acceptance. It wasn't easy. I had to practice all this stuff that I am sharing with you. Things turned around. She is still a free woman as I write today, and I still seek justice, but not revenge. I found this passage online which eloquently sums up where I am: "Justice refers to the process of law where the wrongdoers are judged and punished fairly. Revenge is the act of harming or hurting someone as a punishment for something they have done." The main difference between justice and revenge is their aim; justice aims to right a wrong; whereas, revenge simply aims to get even. So, I personally moved through the grieving process. I cannot be sure that I won't go back into grieving. I continue to rack up losses as we find more and more things that she has done, but forgiving her has allowed me to not be angry, depressed, etc. That decision is less about her and all about me.

Also, I had to stop beating myself up for feeling so bad. That's like chastising a child, expecting that he shouldn't cry when he has lost his mother. Of course, he should. He hurts; thus, he is grieving. So, don't be hard on yourself; allow yourself time to grieve, too. There is no time limit on grieving. Time is relative. Rule of thumb: the deeper the pain, the longer the grieving.

12. Protect Yourself from Further Pain, but Don't Isolate Yourself

A natural response is to push people away when grieving or hurting. But, this is the time to draw people closer to you. You need people who can pour into you and support you. Yet, be sure to protect yourself from further pain. Limit the time you have to spend around the offender. If you work on a project together, continue to meet, but you aren't obligated to go have coffee and chat as if nothing has happened. I need you to know that you can have someone in your life or on the job that sends jabs and friendly fire causing you distress and discomfort. The onus is on you to address it, and if they are unwilling to correct whatever is the situation, then you need to make sure you are out of harm's way. Only you know what this is and what it looks like.

When I moved to Asia, I met a group of trailing wives, women who relocate to follow their husbands' careers overseas. I found out after a few months that one of the ladies was in a dire situation; wherein, her husband had lost his good oil and gas job. Unfortunately, some people are at their best when someone is at her worst. So, a couple of the women took jabs at her and made her last few months in Asia miserable. I couldn't understand why she continued to subject herself to the abuse. She finally stood up for herself by not attending a function where all the women would gather, including the two women who were spiteful and nasty towards her. She was criticized for not going to the "all girls' outing." I'm thinking, why would she place herself in a situation where she was going to be further attacked and harmed? I applauded her for not going.

Forgiveness doesn't mean you owe anyone a pound of flesh, so don't allow yourself to be placed in harm's way. If it means declining invites, etc., so be it. But, I believe you should put your big girl panties on and tell whomever the truth about your decision to limit your time with them. I'm just saying.

I cannot tell you how blessed I am to have had all this misfortune and chaos. Similar to Roberta Guaspari, who found her voice, her way and a passion that led to achieving greatness from despair, I too am finding the silver lining in my clouds. There is no way I would have left America if all was well, but I was pushed out. I write about how people are pushed or pulled into things. Asia didn't necessarily pull me over, I was pushed over. And, I say this without malice or contempt. I can't change what happened, so I find solace in what I've received versus what I lost. I can genuinely thank the people whom I have mentioned or who attempted to cause my demise. You never know what will come out of what was meant for your demise. Okay that's harsh; let me rephrase that. (Read aloud and slowly) You must forgive because what someone did knowingly or unknowingly, may create opportunities that could not otherwise have happened without whatever they did, whether intentionally or unintentionally. I have a dear friend: my BFF (Best Friends Forever). She was my client over 20 years ago at a university where she worked. We stayed in touch through the years and we became friends. The tables turned and, many years later, I asked her to come work for me. It was disastrous. I had to own up to all of it. I contacted her and asked for forgiveness. I know that I placed her in a dire situation because she left a good paying job to join my company. I had no idea that it wasn't going to work so I unintentionally did her harm. But, now she has her own business. She has traveled the world with her business, and now has ownership of her destiny. That would not have happened if she stayed with the original company. I was a conduit. Yes, it hurt and there may still be some ups and downs to her journey, but forgiveness has allowed us to be friends and to be there for one another. Sometimes I think about it and regret what happened because I am truly sorry for how things went south, but at the same time, I was a stepping stone to greater things and not an obstacle for her. What you may see as an obstacle could be a stepping stone if you forgive and not try to change the past. The past is just that: the past. And, that friend is Nona who edited this book, and is mentioned on the Dedication page.

I've shared with you how to forgive people, right? But, what about other forces in circumstances; whereby, you feel wronged? I haven't disclosed how deep I had fallen into a rabbit hole and that I was angry with the world. When someone loses a loved one, it is not uncommon to curse God, would you agree? We hear about people who even turn away from God or have self-loathing. The next section contains insight about that which brought me through.

Forgiving - The All

I have talked about the three storms, which challenged me to forgive my wasband and an ex-employee. I mentioned my near-death experience, but did I share that I was angry with God? I had to forgive God, too. I was angry with God for allowing all of this: from theft to near death. I felt betrayed. I even started to doubt God's existence. I was thinking that if there is a God whom I believed in and whom I served with all my heart and soul, then how could he be so cruel?

I have served my God with love through my talents, tenth (tithing/offering) and time. In one year, I gave $75,000 to nonprofits to help people in a variety of ways. Money was not the only way that I gave, I followed the practice of giving, e.g. donations, scholarships, etc. And, I gave of myself, too. I started a women's ministry in my 30s which was built upon the concept of the Trinity. I selected professional women who were Christians. The premise of the group was spiritual, social and service. We would come together to study the Bible and understand our walk with God. We would go to dinner, theater, etc. to fellowship. The most rewarding aspect for me was the service piece. I challenged the women to gather clothes that they could donate to a shelter including one personal item that they wanted to keep but were willing to give. I coordinated a day long activity at a women's shelter where we each used our gifts/talents to help women. A couple of women stayed with the children and did arts and crafts, a few of us taught job search courses, while a few women did things such as legal advice, etc. Then the ladies who lived in the shelter went to a room to look over the items we brought and selected things that they wanted or needed. It was wonderful. I have years and years of examples of being a good steward during my spiritual journey. Twice, I have given my spiritual center $10,000 during the holidays to support my place of worship. So, between giving money and myself, I felt that I had a special relationship with God. But what really made me feel as if I had a close relationship with God was my walk and faith. I truly believed in God as my all. I knew that everything that I accomplished was based on God's love for me.

But, when things started to unravel, I questioned God's love for me. How can someone who loves me so much allow so many horrible things to happen to me? I felt like Job from the Bible. What kind of God would allow such suffering? I was mad as hell with God (no pun intended). I struggled with believing whether God even loved me. I believed in God, but I started to think that maybe God didn't believe in me. That is what I thought, but, here is what I know:

I used to say that God was always with me. And that God did things either for me, with me or to me. That has now changed. I understand that God does things for me, through me and with me. God does love me and believes in me. In fact, God has not veered from his plans for allowing me to be an instrument of his love for this world. That is why I say that God does things through me. Just maybe God needed me to experience the pain to share with others the meaning of joy and how to be whole even when you feel as if you are falling apart.

Maybe, just maybe, how I saw God was faulty. Maybe God doesn't make things happen. I had to listen over and over to the book, *Why Bad Things Happen to Good People,* by Harold Kushner, a conservative rabbi. I was consumed with trying to understand why a just God would allow me to experience so much suffering. I'm not ashamed to say that the pain was so great and deep that I contemplated suicide. Surely, God could see what he was causing, right? But, what if God doesn't make things happen or even intervene, since we as people have free will? Maybe God loves us and hurts just as much as we do from our suffering. Maybe God gives us people and things in our lives to help us through the storm. A mom doesn't stop the rain shower, but rather provides her child with an umbrella. You may be thinking; what kind of mom would send her child to school in a storm or showers with thunder and dark clouds all around. What we may not know based on our not having to endure poverty is that this mom realizes that her child must go through that storm to get to school to get an education that will give her a way out of poverty. So, she allows her child to go through the storm, but with an umbrella.

I wanted God to stop the pain and then punish those who had hurt me. I wanted revenge. But now, it isn't about revenge, it is about justice: I feel that I must reemphasize. And, in terms of time, it seems like these last four plus years have been a lifetime. But, maybe for God three years is equivalent to 30 minutes because time is relative. Jokingly, I said to my brother that God was at a control console that was basically the world. God could see all the things happening, and occasionally he intervenes, but he's careful to not get too involved because there is a ripple effect. So, he watches the world to make sure nothing gets too far out of hand. Then there is me, a tiny light that represents my life. He sees me and cares for me as well. Then God takes a coffee break to do whatever God does, similar to the seventh day of rest. When he returns, my world has been flipped on its side and turned inside out. My light is dim and hardly flickering. He looks and says, "For Christ's sake, I've only been gone for a minute. What the heck happened?" (Now, that was a pun and a joke, if you didn't catch it.) At any rate, while I'm struggling for years, it is merely seconds for God and it can take merely seconds to repair all the damage that was done. That's the beauty of God. Miracles can happen. Everyone says all that was taken from me will be returned and maybe even multiplied. I couldn't see it or believe that as a reality until now. I know that I will be whole again, and I'm confident that I will receive more than I lost. This battle was not my battle and maybe it wasn't even about me. Maybe God choose me as a conduit. Just maybe God needed to deal with my wasband to see him for who he truly is and to test his heart; and maybe Tammy who claims to be a Christian and outwardly shows her faith needed her soul tested, too. Maybe God thought that I was strong enough and that my faith was wide enough to endure the pain; whereas, someone else may have withered under the pressure. You know, sometimes our parents believe things about us that may not be the case or we can't see it for ourselves. Maybe God thought that I was the perfect vehicle to drive his point and didn't realize that it was too much and too painful for me to handle at the time. And now, God may feel bad about the pain he caused. Isn't God like our earthly parents who feel for us and sometimes make mistakes? Now, that is a hard pill to swallow. God, making mistakes? I don't know. But, I do know that what has happened, and what I endured, I did not deserve: good or bad.

I didn't deserve the blessings of wealth, but I also didn't deserve what people did to me. So, for me…I had to forgive God. So, yes, I forgave God. Isn't that what you do when you are angry with others for what you believe they have done to you? I've been able to forgive myself and for the past year, I vacillated between forgiveness and revenge for Tammy and others. But, overall, I'm in a space of forgiveness. I forgave God, whether he believes it is warranted or whether anyone else believes it is necessary. There was a woman who couldn't understand how I could say that God needs forgiving when God makes no mistakes. That is a falsehood for me. But, that is my belief based on my need to find meaning in it all. God is not all knowing because we have free will. I believe our heart and minds are known but how others may impact us may come as a shock, even to God. And, God's way of doing something for us may actually hurt us more than what was considered. This is just my way of attempting to understand something that is much greater than me.

In closing on this line of thought, here is my humble attempt to share with you how I forgave the main characters in my horror story, God and myself. Wikipedia states, "Forgiveness is the intentional and voluntary process by which a victim undergoes a change in feelings and attitude regarding an offense, let go of negative emotions such as vengefulness, with an increased ability to wish the offender well." As for knowing that I have forgiven God, I have. I had to realize that God loved me and that all things are done for my highest and greatest good. Once I came to terms with myself regarding what God is and is not in my life, I was able to have a better understanding of why things happen or do not happen. I cannot be angry with God for something others do. I was displacing my anger and blaming the wrong source for my frustration. Being angry with God caused me to start hating and murder plotting. I became consumed with revenge to the point I didn't recognize myself any more. The angrier I became, the sadder I felt. I was consumed with pain and resentment. I just wanted it to go away by holding on. Now, does that make sense? No. I share this with you so that you can come to terms with your beliefs to better understand why you may feel the way that you feel. How you feel is paramount as the earlier quote indicates "…undergoes a change in feelings…" What you may be feeling stems from your spiritual/religious beliefs that may run counter to your healing.

The Ultimate Act of Forgiveness: Self-Forgiveness

When it came to me forgiving, I needed to forgive the offenders, God and then myself, which was the most difficult of all. There had to be blame and once forgiveness takes place, the blame game is over. Ironically, I had to stop blaming myself and then I could forgive myself. I became infuriated with myself for trusting, for being fooled, for losing my wealth and the list goes on and on, right? It was important to know that I was the victim, not the victimizer. I should not and did not have to blame myself. There was enough blaming to go around.

Then, I felt a deep sense of shame. But, let me tell you something. Shame keeps us hostage. I didn't discuss the perfect storm with people until I came to terms with what happened and began working towards forgiveness. I felt such shame about everything, so much so that I didn't reach out to government agencies like the U.S. Secret Service that deals with embezzlement and where I have relationships because I didn't want to explain what happened and be considered a failure. Then my brother, the retired police officer, shared with me that I was the victim and had no reason to be ashamed. That is when I was able to put things in perspective. I now know that you must give up the guilt, the shame, the anger, disappointment, etc., which means letting go.

To forgive yourself means to accept that you are human and to recognize that everything that occurred, whether due to your fault or someone else's actions is in the past. You cannot change that, but you can change how you respond to it. I adopted and practiced the same techniques that I mentioned earlier with a little extra step. I started thinking positive thoughts. When I would lay down at night, sometimes I could not sleep although I was exhausted. I would play out various scenes over and over as if I were a director with the power to cut out scenes, leaving huge chunks of tapes on the editing floor. But it never worked. I would just lie there obsessing on what I could have done differently. I started doing a simple thing to break that train of thought. I would lie down, close my eyes and say positive words. Depending on how deep in the rabbit hole you have gone, you may be unable to think of many words, initially. So, I would think the words or say slowly with deliberation, "Joy, peace, happy, harmony, tranquility, relaxation, serenity, love…." Within time, I would drift off to sleep. This is the same practice as counting sheep, which hasn't been scientifically proven or disproven to work. I have found that imagining or saying positive words by pausing between each word creates a soothing effect and it has worked for others to whom I've recommended the technique. Over time, I had an extensive list of words that I couldn't get through before falling asleep to wake up refreshed. This minimized negative thoughts and filled my subconscious with positivity. That must occur before you can even begin forgiving yourself. You must get rid of the negativity that surrounds you and fills your thoughts. Then, and only then, are you truly free.

Doubling Down: Turning the Tables

Now, that you've forgiven, it's time to work on being forgiven. When managing and leading you are gonna break some eggs. During a significant phase of owning my business, I was a terror instead of being an exceptional leader. I was rarely unjust or inaccurate in my assessment of people; however, I was sometimes harsh. When I learned to lead, I turned a new leaf. I even went desk to desk and apologized to several employees whom I might have offended at one time or another. In fact, I was able to reach out to some past employees and apologize, a part of the 12-step process that I advocate. One step to recovery is to apologize as long as it doesn't do more harm. So, I would call former employees who I know didn't feel whole when they left my company. Unfortunately, I didn't know who all was either positively or negatively impacted. So, some people weren't contacted and others did not come up on my conscious radar. Things were going very well for me and I started to blog. Within a few weeks, I started getting these very disturbing emails or comments on my blog. What the hell? Why does this old employee keep writing this stuff as a rebuttal to everything that I said? Not only would she comment on my blogs, but she would find anything written about me, dissect it and berate me. I didn't realize it, but this was the true definition of a disgruntled employee. I could see that she was miserable. In truth, I wasn't the source of her frustration, but I was a reminder of past disappointments, etc. so she would lash out at me. Every Sunday, she would comment on my blog by addressing every line with an attack or example of how I had been a terrible leader. At first, I ignored her, but then I finally sat down and wrote to her. I started with a heartfelt apology and explained my failure to be a good leader due to my lack of knowledge and misperceptions regarding how to lead. She didn't respond, but she stopped writing the three-page letters every Sunday. She merely wanted what everyone wants, and that is to be understood, valued and respected, which are things she didn't receive while under my leadership as an employee. I gave them to her as a former employee. Remember that it is never too late to seek forgiveness just as it is never too late to give forgiveness.

Seeking Forgiveness

When I truly started my journey of growth, I started recognizing the need to make amends and basically atone. For several years, I made a list of anyone whom I thought I might have harmed in one way or another. The first year or two, the list was long, and now I don't have a list. This is not because I don't do harm, at least not knowingly. I'm human so I can't please everyone which means someone is not going to be happy. But, the difference between the new woman and the old me is that I resolve conflict as soon as possible and apologize quickly when required. I'm cognizant about treating people with a level of respect and love that promotes a healthy relationship. I didn't understand this when I was younger or before I worked on developing leadership skills. Now, I'm more inclined to deal with things immediately versus letting them drag out and fester. During my mid-career stage, I started a practice that I felt was beneficial. Each year as the year was ending and the new year was beginning, I would contact people to say that I was sorry and even ask for their forgiveness.

One year, I tracked down an old boss who had fired me and did some things that were unfair and borderline unethical. But, I was no saint, either. I didn't go quietly into the night. We were mutual career women and professional friends before she hired me. She asked me to do things that were unreasonable, and she kept stealing my ideas and taking the credit. That was pissing me off. I started making waves and I went over her head to her boss to complain (an unwritten rule to not do). I knew that such was politically incorrect, but I had grown tired of her. She asked me to resign and as I exited, I complained about her at the highest level.

Well, after a few years, I started thinking about my actions. Just because someone uses tactics that are not above board doesn't mean I have to do things to match their style or behavior. She had since left that organization. So, I contacted someone who was able to get in touch with her. The colleague wouldn't give me her number because she remembered how contentious that relationship and my departure were for all parties. She said that she would call my old boss to let her know that I was looking to connect. This was way before social media. I got her email address a week or two later and I emailed her an apology about how I left the job and how I behaved. I got a phone call within minutes. She was on the other end and I could hear that sound that people make when they cry. You know the sniffling sound? She expressed how appreciative she was of my email and that she wanted to apologize for how she treated me. She even said that she understood why I did what I did because she caused me to do so. I didn't see that coming. Fortuitously, my actions opened the door for her to apologize, which is a step in the forgiveness process, and to let go of something she had been carrying as well. I was fortunate because sometimes you may not have the chance to apologize or right a wrong. Heck, we are all just people trying to do our best with no absolute instructions that came in our box of life.

I believe seeking forgiveness runs a close second to forgiving. Just as we should forgive, it is honorable to seek forgiveness. For some, it may be more difficult to do one or the other, while both may be an uphill battle for most. Some of this boils down to having a moral compass and professional integrity, which equal career maturity. But, with any of this, it's about choices. I just can't see how anyone can have the audacity to be on their high horse and practice forgiveness but not ask for forgiveness. Could it be that forgiving gives people the upper hand and causes them to feel as if they are in control while asking for forgiveness makes one feel powerless? I believe you should exercise both for sustainable success and happiness.

Seeking forgiveness is a four-part process:

The problem with the whole notion of apologies and forgiveness is that people often don't feel that they have done anything wrong. What if we think about it like this? If I do something for my kids and it causes embarrassment, yet it was for their good, do I need their forgiveness for how I made them feel and not necessarily for what I did? I'm just thinking. Some people do things and feel that they were right, and refuse to apologize, but you may still need to forgive even though they don't accept fault. Forgiveness is not about them but your willingness to see their imperfections and faults and dismiss them as human frailty. The reverse is true. We need to be seen for our humanness. Here are four steps that will help others forgive you:

1. **Acknowledge the Offense**

    This can be difficult if you really don't know what you have done. But, let's be real, if you are a sentient being, you can usually figure out what you've done to someone. You may not agree on whether they should be mad or as mad about it, but you have a feel for when you've done something wrong. The problem is usually our ego doesn't allow us to think that we can be in the wrong. So, we justify our actions. But, you know what? Just stop it. As Mark Twain said, "A man is never more truthful than when he acknowledges himself a liar." Don't lie to yourself about things that have impacted others. I hear people make excuses for others saying that they just don't have the capacity to empathize or understand. No, I gotta call horse *^$% on that. Even a dog knows when he has done something wrong. He will tuck his tail when he sees you. If a dog has awareness, surely a professional person has awareness, too. So, yes, you as a professional know when you have done something that can negatively impact others. And, you must own up to it, first to yourself, and then to whomever was impacted. I believe that you must articulate what occurred. For example, state that what you did was xyz, e.g. hurtful, harmful, selfish, mean spirited, unfair, etc., right? That levels the playing field and places context around what is being discussed so that all parties are on the same page with the same understanding. The person may acknowledge that you are on point or say that such wasn't a problem and then you can decide to still apologize based on how you feel, or let it go. Also, the person can articulate what was the actual transgression in his/her eyes. This is not about you, but rather how the other person was impacted. You may find what s/he says and/or recalls are slightly different from your recollection. Attempt to find a mutually agreed upon understanding of the event/situation.

2. **Offer an Explanation of the Offense**

    Don't give an excuse, but rather an explanation. Now what is the difference? According to Psyche Central, "Excuses deny responsibility while explanations allow for responsibility to be acknowledged, and the situation to be explored and understood. Excuses come from feelings of defensiveness that pop up when someone is feeling attacked, while explanations occur when someone wants to be understood." So, don't give an excuse which is often wrapped in falsehood to some extent, to persuade someone that you were justified. Instead, be authentic about why you did what you did, or why you didn't do what you should have done.

3. **Express Remorse or Even Shame**

    I know, this isn't easy for anyone with any legitimate level of pride. But think of it this way: use the Sunshine Rule. If light were to shine on what happened and all could see your deeds, especially those whom you honor and respect, and you value how they view you, would you be okay or shamed that they saw that action or deed? It can be easy not to have shame or remorse when only you and maybe the other person are the only ones who know of your deeds. But, widen the lens and allow the light to shine in. Are you still okay or do you recognize there should be some shame? If so, humble yourself and express that shame or remorse. It can be as simple as saying that you regret that you insulted them; however, unintentional but, yet it happened, and you feel xyz.

4. **Offer a Reparation or Statement to Not Repeat the Offense**

    Sometimes just a heartfelt apology is more than enough. But go a step further. Atone by offering to replace what was lost. If it was money, that is easy to figure out. If it is face, then what can you do to give that person something you took. Say it was an idea that you took and did not attribute to someone else. Then allow that person to present the next idea or go back and notify others that you failed to mention that Mary actually came up with the idea. There are so many ways to make amends. But, I find the most effective way is to simply ask Mary, "What would you like to see happen?" or "How can I right this for you?" Again, the apology is usually more than enough but she may ask that you write a retraction or a letter on her behalf expressing how she has great ideas, etc. You may be surprised to find out what people really want when asked. If you can do it, good; do it. If you find that you just entered a quagmire, understand that some people will take advantage of your goodwill. At that point, end the discussion with the heartfelt apology for what happened and that you even regret that you can't make amends, but they can rest assured that it won't happen again. You did your part. You extended the olive branch.

Here are a few additional closing thoughts about granting forgiveness. You may think that you have forgiven someone, but when reminded of the act or person, the feelings and pain associated with that person will resurface. Forgiveness does not mean forgetting, nor does it mean condoning or excusing offenses. In essence, there is forgiveness from a religious/spiritual standpoint and psychological. I say this because it is the intention behind the forgiveness, but at the end of the day it's all about letting go. Some people forgive to be forgiven while others forgive to simply move on. In either case, not forgiving or letting go is like a cancer eating at you. Also, forgiveness requires some humility. Be not proud!

Once a minister told a story that I still carry with me. There was an eagle so proud and fierce that he would swoop down to catch its prey. Every day, the eagle would soar high into the sky towards its nest to partake of its meal. Once it captured a badger in its claws and began to make an ascent to its nest. As the bird of prey flapped its wings and held the badger close to its chest, similar to the way we hold hurt and pain close to our heart, the bird fell from the sky. What had happened was that the badger had chewed through to the eagle's heart. The message in the story is to be so very careful of what we hold onto, especially if it's close to our heart. We sometimes hold the hurt, pain and stuff that impacts us negatively close to our chest as if it is a part of our life support or as a badge of honor, right? It's as if we say to others, "Look how good I am, based on how very bad this person is, based on what they did to me." The badge can be many things to different people. Holding on is sometimes easier than letting go, while entertaining revenge is far more satisfying than forgiveness; until, you realize that it is killing you! Similar to McCourt's quote on resentment written earlier in this chapter is another quote, "Holding onto anger is like drinking poison and expecting the other person to die." This quote is attributed to Buddha, Gandhi, Mandela and others. There is no evidence of who first said it, but allow me to rewrite it as well. It is soooo damn hard to let go when the pain is so deep, right? Everyone talks about forgiveness; however, people don't seem to practice it in the workplace where it is needed most. I hope you are starting to feel inclined to practice this act.

A Proper Letting Go

Now that we've explored forgiveness with an appropriate amount of insight, let's talk about letting go. The story about the eagle deals with pride, but it also embodies the importance of letting go. Letting go is far more difficult to understand because it can be confused with the act of forgetting. People assume that if you let something go then you should forget about the act or deed. But, no. It's not one and the same. You can forgive, let go, but remember what happened. In my opinion, that only makes sense. If we forget things such as wars, conflict, betrayal, affairs and whatever, it is bound to happen again. We remember for two reasons: (1) to understand what happened and (2) to learn from it. And, maybe, just maybe, to honor what was achieved from it such as memorials, a date of someone's death, etc. Sometimes, we find solace in remembering what got us from there to here. For example, when my oldest son, Russell, was coming of age, I purchased a book titled, "Lest We Forget: The Passage from Africa to Slavery and Emancipation," by Velma Maia Thomas. It is a powerful 3D interactive book that tells our story, i.e. blacks brought over from Africa to America in bondage. It is not about hate or anything that would remotely resemble revenge. It's about remembrance of who we are and how we arrived in a foreign land to physically build the financial foundation to what we now know as America. It's about our history that we should never forget, while we forgive and let go of the pain, hurt and anger associated with those very dark times. If you have gotten as far as forgiving, what purpose does it serve to hold on to it versus releasing it? Why are we so compelled to hold on to what obviously causes distress? Letting go is merely the final act in forgiving; however, not essential but highly recommended. But, let me reemphasize, letting go is not, nor should it be, about forgetting.

As mentioned earlier, we often hear about letting go, but no one has fully or succinctly told me what that actually means when I ask. This has been the most traumatic four plus years of my life. Now, check this out! These were supposed to be the golden years when I turned 50 and as I prepared to retire. Instead of receiving a watch, I've been completely traumatized, and the comforting advice that I continued to hear was "Let it go." Let go of what? Let go of the future that I had planned for myself? Let go of the love and lovers I lost? Hell! Let go of my company that was my identity, or better yet, let go of my identity that was stolen? Let go of desiring the lifestyle to which I had become accustomed? What? What all must I let go of to feel normal, loved and whole again? Let go of the mounds and mounds of betrayal? But, what if the pain is all you have left? How do you let go of that? How do you let go of the fury that fuels you to continue, and why should you? Well, in my case, it is because it was destroying me; it was causing me to be someone I didn't recognize or want to be. I had to let go so that I could move on with my life.

At the onset of my storm, my middle son sent me a picture because I was in a dark place, but I didn't know why at that time. So, he sent me a picture of Jesus kneeling in front of a little girl who was holding on tightly to a raggedy old teddy bear. Jesus was asking the little girl for her teddy bear while he held behind his back a huge new cuddly teddy bear to give to her. The little girl response was, "But I love it so." Sometimes we refuse to let go of something for a variety of reasons, even when we are being placed in a position to receive something better. That's letting go when you no longer fear what you don't know, no longer feel pain that is debilitating, and you trust that all will be well. Here is what I think, and this is what I know: letting go requires a few things:

1. **Know That You Deserve Better**

   For you to let go of something that no longer serves a purpose in your life or holds you back means that you must believe that you deserve better. Often, we become so comfortable in mediocrity that we start to believe that what we got is good enough or there isn't anything better. In this case, don't think it or feel it, but rather know it. Know that you deserve better. When I went through some romantic woes with this guy who I was dating, a girlfriend in Tucson, Arizona, gave me a pep talk after I told her what was happening. When I went to visit her, she said to me, "You didn't deserve that, and he doesn't deserve you." That was one of the most profound things that I had heard that allowed me to let go. I now say that to other people who come to me broken from relationships derailed by misdeeds, unkind words, etc.

2. **Trust**

   You must place your trust in yourself, and depending on your belief system, something greater than yourself. That means you must come face-to-face with your faith. This is where your faith will be challenged and called upon. If you haven't stepped out on the limb before, but rather picked the low hanging fruit, or if you have resorted to just gathering fruit that had fallen to the ground, then crawling or leaning out on the limb can be a scary proposition. I have a picture of a little boy. There are four picture frames of this little boy going down a slide. His face has the look of sheer terror as he tries to brace himself and even stop. The caption reads, "When you know it's God's plan, but you're still scared." What we know is that he will be fine and that someone is probably at the bottom of the slide to catch him. Or worst case, he'll merely get to the end and have to either scoot off the edge or he lands on his butt, but he'll survive: that we know. "Trust the process," is what they kept telling my cohort when I was working on my Ph.D. I still can't believe I made it through that program. It was tough! It was right up there with being in the U.S. Marine Corps boot camp, but it was intellectual versus physical torture. I trusted the process: I wrote my dissertation, defended my dissertation and walked across the stage to receive my degree. What in your life is calling you to trust in something other than yourself, or to just trust the process? Trust that letting go will be exactly what you need.

3. Courage

Better to have the devil you know than the possibility of something worse is a well-known belief or practice. It really takes courage to let go because holding on usually stems from possessing either a profound or a hint of fear, especially of the unknown. In either case, it prevents you from moving on, which is what letting go allows you to do. Think of it like this. If you are holding on to a rope, you can only go as far as the rope's length, but if you let go, there is no limit to how far you can and will go. When I coach people through transformational change, I will ask the question, "What's the worst?" I always get the confused look. I ask the question of them, again. Then I explain that I want them to think about the worst-case scenario. Usually, the dreaded worse is so remote a possibility that they discover they are already in a realistic worst-case scenario. So, nothing more can be as bad. We all know what the cowardly lion asked of the wizard in *The Wizard of Oz*. He asked for courage, which he already possessed. My dear, you already have courage, too. You must step into what will release you and you'll discover levels and layers of courage.

Our life encompasses personal and professional aspects. We are faced with situations and circumstances that can cut to our very core. There are things that may cause us to question our sanity, beliefs and even all the choices we have made along the way. I look at the last four years to examine how I got here. What winds blew me to this shore and what storms have I encountered that pushed me or pulled me to the life I am now living? I discovered a few general truths that are the basis of this book. It is easier to recommend to people how to weather a storm than to go through a storm. I have built my practice around coaching and advising people on how to weather the storm. My second book has a chapter that discusses resilience, but I could have never imagined the storms that I have encountered since writing that book. And, living it is much harder than writing about it. Here is what I think, and this is what I know about resilience, forgiveness and letting go, based on my journey: Resilience will carry you through. Forgiveness is the ultimate cure. And, letting go is really your only option for a sense of freedom from pain whether you stay and take it, stay and change it, or leave.

I've had many journeys as I was pushed and pulled in many directions. But, I arrived at destination that works well for me, and where I ultimately wanted to be, but was too afraid to explore. The journey that I am now prepared to talk and write about is the last four plus years. Just as I reached the pinnacle of success and turned my company into a thriving multi-million dollar business, the perfect storm landed on my personal and professional shore. I believe that I came out of the divorce relatively unscathed. There were some minor dents and bruises, but I believed that I could continue to move forward. I still had my company and something I've never had before: freedom. But, then I lost that too. When combining everything, I had to do some heavy lifting: forgiveness and letting go.

Word to the Wise

When you let go of anger or a debilitating feeling that prevents you from being whole or happy, you will gain a sense of peace even through the storm. Forgiveness and letting go allows you to recognize the pain you suffered without letting the pain define you, enabling you to heal and move on. It can free you to be happy. Research reveals that unhappy, angry and hostile people have a challenging time forgiving, even after prolonged periods of time. However, forgiveness improves your health and minimizes stress, strengthens immune system, etc. Thus, the phrase: "He makes me sick!" Not forgiving and holding on to something can make you sick as my story of nearly dying demonstrates. But, the return on that investment is that it frees you from a cell with no walls or lock. In other words, you are free to leave the cell anytime you choose.

When moving forward from mistakes or deeds that need forgiving, I do suggest that you evaluate whether it is a heart mistake or head mistake. A heart mistake is when someone does something knowingly without care or regard for others. Doing something with ill will comes from the heart which is an emotional act. That person didn't care how it would impact you. A head mistake is to make a mistake unknowingly because the person did not understand or know something. A head mistake is when he didn't think through his actions carefully, didn't utilize good decision-making skills, or lacked knowledge, resources or support. But, a heart mistake is when he acts without taking you or the company into consideration, or purposely sabotaged or sought individual gain at your or the company's expense. Once you can determine where something came or stemmed from, you can then not only let go but make better decisions on how you will handle that act. A heart mistake requires a different treatment compared to a head mistake: it is ultimately up to you to decide what you will or will not do. I can move past a head mistake because you can make whatever the person did into a teachable moment. It's difficult to impart wisdom from heart mistakes because those are often malicious, and you will have difficulty changing hearts.

In short, using forgiveness and letting go, as tools for success, will benefit you. Depending on where you are in your career, you have been or will be negatively impacted and how you choose to deal with it will have long-term consequences. Some of those consequences will not be obvious. You may not even know that something occurring in your life stems from not forgiving a colleague. You may develop an unhealthy outlook on relationships based on what someone else did to you and so forth.

Exercise:

Write down incidents that come to mind that caused you discomfort, anger, etc. Hopefully, the list is short but be honest with yourself. Then write down the name that is attached to each situation/circumstance. Evaluate whether it was a heart or head mistake, then write down what or how things would improve if you forgive and just let go. If you can't, you simply just can't do it, at least for now. Be honest with yourself about why. Ask yourself, what am I gaining by not forgiving and letting go and what am I losing, as well? Now, ask yourself, what do you want? Sometimes we aren't clear on what we want. Do you want an apology, acknowledgement, etc.? Be clear on what you want. Then use some of my suggestions, such as contacting them to forgive,

or just forgive in your heart and mind without anyone else knowing but yourself. Check off each person as you either forgive or let go. And, revisit this list until all the names are eventually checked off.

Lastly, how will you even know when forgiveness has been accomplished. I knew that I had forgiven my wasband when I sent him a WhatsApp message applauding him for being a good father and since then we talk every now and then, mostly about the criminal embezzlement case and our sons. As an oh by the way, he didn't receive the entire half-million. I held back $60,000 because I supposedly ran out of money. Oddly enough, Tammy advised me that we couldn't pay him the last two installments. In hindsight, she wanted that money in order to move it into her account. So, in essence, she stole from him, too. In fact, my CPA has termed this whole thing as Tammy Gate, similar to Nixon's Watergate incident that toppled his political career as the President and led him to resign before being impeached.

Back to knowing when forgiveness occurs. I have no idea how Tammy Gate will end. The criminal case against her could lead to a few years of prison time for her and then again maybe nothing will happen, which would be a disheartening blow because that would mean justice wasn't served. In either case, I will have to be ok with it since I have forgiven and let go of the incident, as much as is humanly possible. But, I must reiterate that forgiveness doesn't mean that you don't want justice. Of course, I want justice. I believe she should have to deal with the consequences of her actions. But, forgiveness releases me from the pain, anger, sleeplessness and a host of other emotions, negative thoughts and feelings that ride shot gun alongside of me when I haven't forgiven someone. You can be disappointed with someone and still forgive them. Forgiveness in its simplest form is to not be tied to the emotions, shame, pain, etc. caused by someone or an action. It doesn't mean you say, "Well, they set my house on fire. No need to call the fire department. Let's forget this ever happened." No! You call the fire department, you attempt to salvage what you can, you seek justice and then you move through the emotions that you will experience from your losses, and you forgive the arsonists which is to not to let them off the hook per se but rather to not allow them or the situation to have control over your emotions.

It's letting go of the narrative, the passage, the shit that has you stuck: that's forgiveness. I don't use profanity to shock you, but there simply isn't a word that embodies all that I have gone through and what many professionals encounter in their career. If you are fortunate enough, you can then work on "letting it go." I don't foresee recovering the money she stole even though a court awarded me nearly one million dollars. I'm working as hard as ever to rebuild my life, but I'm happy. That is all that really matters at this point. If I was not in a place of forgiveness, I would cringe every time I heard her name because I'm forced to relive many unfortunate situations that I must contend with as a result of her misdeeds.

A businesswoman asked me to coach her, based on my past accomplishments. I asked her to tell me what she wanted to achieve. She was quick to explain that she wanted to make money and that she didn't earn enough despite all her efforts. I looked at her and asked whether that was really what she wanted or something else. She was flabbergasted as she explained how she should be making sooo much money. I must have looked puzzled because she then asked me what I wanted. I looked at her and said, "Joy. I want joy." And, that is ultimately what you acquire, achieve or receive when you forgive and let go: joy.

I know emphatically that I have forgiven and let go of the things that caused my perfect storm. Here is one way that lets me know that I have forgiven. I used to disclose the incident only to people whom I trusted. Now, I openly explain why I'm in Asia to anyone who asks, yeah. The first three years, I would cry whenever I would tell the story, and those I was speaking to would cry as well. Now, I smile because it's so surreal that it's almost laughable. But, here is what I had to take notice of: recently, I shared my story with a guy who I met online, right? We met up and he said that he Googled me. Okay, people do that, yeah. Then he looked at me in a way to say, I'm going to ask you something that you may not be comfortable answering. He proceeded to say, "I see that you were very successful in the US, and now you are here," as he looked around as if to point out that we were in Asia. He implied that I had a story, but he also made a facial gesture that seemed to suggest that I had something to hide because he said, "This doesn't add up. Why are you here?" He mentioned that my age, background, being Black, my gender, and other attributes are not typically found in Asia; so, what gives, right? Just a year ago, I would have given a story that was true but not complete. I would have said that my divorce had wreaked havoc which seemed more palatable. But, I shared with him my perfect storms. There was a time when I would have had tears in my eyes discussing what I held close to the chest, but I was animated through the entire story and at the end of my story, I smiled. He had a hard time wrapping his head around the story because I was smiling. So, I shared with him that I have forgiven people, myself, etc. He expressed concern and even sorrow. He kept telling me how sorry he was for me. I was like, "Baby, don't be sorry for

Chapter 4: Forgiveness and Letting Go: A Game Changer

me. I have a great life and gained more than I lost. It's fine; I'm blessed." That confused him even more. But, what it said to me is that I've let it go and I'm no longer mentally, physically or spiritually impacted by those storms. I'm coming out of the storm.

When is it over? Forgiving and letting go doesn't mean that it is over and that you won't ever feel whatever you are feeling or even thinking. As a mere mortal, you can be triggered by something. Think of this thing, i.e. storm, event or act, as a very hot pot that you pick up. The pot is the deed that needed your forgiveness. If you are burned by that pot, but you let it go by either dropping it or placing it in the sink, you will have a burning sensation for as little as a minute or much longer, accompanied by blisters. But, you let go of the pot, i.e. incident so you will heal, right? However, for some reason you pick up a hot pot again; maybe the same pot or a different pot, and you may experience the same pain. Why do we pick up the pot again? Who knows…maybe interacting with that pot isn't such a good idea or maybe it's a new set of pots and we are triggered by that memory. Don't beat yourself up because you relived the incident or started thinking about that pain (pot) is what I'm saying. It doesn't mean that you didn't forgive or you didn't let go. Unfortunately, it means you picked it back up. You simply need not dwell on whatever thoughts you are having and let whatever you feel to simply pass through you without judgement or guilt. In short, you may have to let it go again. I woke up one morning and started thinking about what ifs and I could see my mind going down the proverbial rabbit hole. So, I quickly saw the person and incident as a hot pot. I dropped it, i.e. the pot in my mind and I instantly disconnected from the thoughts. I sat up and began my day on a positive note. I love this stuff: it works.

I must stop writing or I'll continue writing about this and we must let go and move on, yeah. If you want to read more, get the next book, which will cover everything in more detail in hopes of becoming a screenplay. In the last chapter, I quoted Haruki Murakami, "That's what this storm's all about.," I would like to end with my own statement on what this is all about:

"To move from shame to sharing, from fear to forgiveness, and from pain to power. That's what my perfect storm was all about!"

Dr. Indigo

Chapter 5

The Practicality of Spirituality

Allow me to level set before I share what I think and what I know about the practical use of spirituality in the workplace. When I Googled the question - What is spirituality? This is one of the many definitions: *the quality of being concerned with the human spirit or soul as opposed to material or physical things.* Then I wanted to see what is regarded as spirit because I use the word spirit and spirituality in a general and not in a religious sense. For example, we hear, "In the spirit of giving" or "That's the spirit", etc. *Spirit can mean relating to or affecting the human essence or soul. Spirit is the non-physical part of a person which is the seat of emotions and character; the soul.*

Bruce Lee who I consider to be one of the most prolific thought leaders and philosophers of my generation said, "Self-knowledge involves relationship. To know oneself is to study oneself in action with another person. Relationship is a process of self-evaluation and self-revelation." I believe spirituality is the relationship between you and the source which is revealed in relationships with others. When I speak of source, that is an entity from which you are able to draw power, energy, calmness, strength, peace, joy, etc. It is that which you recognize as greater than yourself but also a part of self. Based on my personal belief, this is God whom I often refer to as *The All*. A relationship with something greater than yourself shouldn't be reserved or assigned to a specific day but practiced daily. I don't care who you are, what you do or where you do it; you will have moments in your life where you will drop to your knees to either pray or catch yourself from falling. Okay, that was a little melodramatic. I'm speaking from personal experience, based on the many disruptions in my life, from nearly dying twice to the betrayal that caused me to lose my business and almost my mind. I want to get your attention to share with you what carried me through and to compel you to tap into that something to carry you through the storms of life or your career. However, I believe we short change ourselves when we don't go to the well until we are thirsty. What if you developed a relationship that is continual so that you have balance and all the things you desire consistently?

Like any relationship, it takes effort. When we have an accepting and loving relationship with self, it will allow us to have better relationships with others. This can be achieved with a spiritual foundation that is manifested through a variety of practices, i.e. activities. Trust me, you are going to need it, if you haven't thus far. If you are in a storm right now, may this chapter answer questions you have yet to ask and serve as a compass in your situation. If you are fine and everything is coming up roses, read this chapter for future answers to questions you will one day ask.

I couldn't write about anything until I wrote about this: spirituality. Even though it is in the back of the book, it was written first. What you read throughout the book was not for the faint of heart. I shared my story from a four-year perspective, giving you a front row seat to storms that would have blown me away if not for the spiritual practice(s) and beliefs that kept me grounded. A common message throughout this book is about weathering the storm, yeah. But, it's about so much more. It's about finding your way. So, curl up with a glass of wine and continue to allow yourself to take this walk of redemption, freedom and enlightenment with me to help you manage your life and career more effectively. Spirituality is something that can be practiced daily to energize yourself like drinking a cup of coffee in the morning, or to level set at the end of the day. I don't want to give the impression that you need spirituality only when the crap hits the fan. Spirituality techniques are practical enough to practice daily for balance, and God knows that we can get off balanced by the stuff people say and do whether intentionally or unintentionally. In fact, we can wake up on the right side of the bed and then have a heated discussion with our significant other which will lead people to think that we got up on the wrong side of the bed when you show up for work. Within the time frame of a couple of hours, our attitude and mood can plummet due to a conversation that we had at home and carried into the workplace. Unfortunately, there are some things we just can't place in our briefcase until we get back home.

This chapter is for everyone, whether you are an atheist or the follower of one religion or another. Interestingly, I was sharing with a friend, who is an atheist, about my passion and purpose around spirituality and asked him whether he has ever heard a small voice inside that comforts or guides him. He looked at me and shook his head. I tried to explain that I was referring to a spiritual thing and not to religion. He wasn't biting. So, for clarity. What this chapter will introduce are practices and techniques that range from rejuvenating you anytime of the day to comforting you when you may become stressed. Now, I know even atheists become stressed, right? In essence, this chapter is about maintaining balance or space that keeps you from choking the hell out of someone at work when you've had enough (smile).

Here is what I think, and this is what I know about spirituality. I am where I am and alive because I went within for understanding and healing. God is within me. Of course, I spoke to therapists, friends, family and colleagues. Let's be real: as a part of my healing process, I spoke to anyone willing to listen to the bits and pieces I was willing to divulge. I wrap my spiritual belief into almost everything because it is the foundation of my strength, purpose and being. Nearly 20 years ago, I used to have on my business card, "Learn to listen to your inner voice for it is God whispering to your soul." I had a client come to me and say that I was denied an opportunity to speak at an event because the panel thought that my card indicated that I was too religious. I had to laugh because I'm not religious at all: I'm spiritual. So, what's the difference? My electronic sage, Google, routed me to a website titled *The Question* that revealed an article written by Steven Harsant who said, "Spirituality gives the individual autonomy over his or her interpretation of the soul or spirit, whereas religion implies participation in a communal practice and interpretation of divine belief and worship." I once heard that you can have spirituality with the absence of religion, but you rarely have religion with the absence of spirituality. I'm spiritual and not religious because my belief and practices are sacred and something special that I have with my God. I do not impose my God on others, but I do offer understanding about circumstances that I have worked through, based on my spirituality.

In this chapter, I must give another disclaimer, which is that I embrace all religions but practice none. I respect everyone's belief and religion as their truth and I honor the divinity in all. Some refer to this as Oneness. I believe that we are all connected, but certain things separate us. So, read this chapter with an understanding that it is not grounded in any particular religion, but rather on a level of truth for me to help you grow. I may state things from a Christian point of view based on my upbringing, or Buddhism, which is an awesome practice; or whatever seems to apply to the situation. So, I ask that you keep an open mind and take what works for you and leave whatever doesn't for the next person.

While living in a Muslim country, I'm often asked about my beliefs. Religion around the world has become a preoccupation, even a qualifier or sadly, a disqualifier. I meet well-meaning people who ask me whether I'm Christian if they are Christian, or whether I'm Muslim, if they are Muslim, and so forth. I simply reply that I embrace all religions but practice none. I mean, what more can you really want from someone? Wouldn't you want someone to simply embrace others' beliefs, regardless of what they practice or don't practice? I could go on a tangent and explain that I was a Christian, that I thought I was called to the ministry and I was going to work on my doctorate in Divinity, but I didn't want to lead a church; and then I thought that I would get my doctorate in Theology, but I didn't want to learn Latin. Whew, I have always known that I had a calling to serve God, but I refuse to place a label on God's awesomeness. I believe that God and the Universe are one and expresses its greatness (no word can capture what I'm saying) through us. This is my disclaimer: I will refer to God, reference a variety of prophets and divine spirits in sayings, quotes, etc. I am not saying that one is more of the truth than the other. I may draw upon stories to emphasize a point. You are welcome to change the name that I use to a name that you recognize. The messenger simply is not as important as the message itself. Give me some grace and forgiveness to share with you what works for me. I have been at this game for a long time and I can say that if it weren't for my faith and practices, I would not be where I am or how I am. I'm not where and exactly who I need to be but thank God I'm not what I used to be; this allows me to play the game with integrity and with a compass pointing to 'my' true north.

You may be asking what in the hell (no pun intended) does this chapter have to do with the game. This book is about the game and the unwritten rules, right? What is interesting is that prior to a start of a game, whether football, baseball or whatever, nearly every organized sport has a prayer said with the team in formation, or a moment of silence. That is not a part of the sport itself or even in the rule book, but it is an unwritten rule that team members observe. I believe just as an athlete acknowledges the divine power or source, so should I if I want to move through my day or situations with greater ease and grace. Let's face it, the workplace can be brutal. It can feel as if you are in a true rugby game when trying to get someone with influence to adopt your idea or project. And, during your appraisal when you are asking for an increase in pay or even meaningful responsibilities you can feel as if you are in a wrestling match. Good grief. Unless you're in the military, going to work should not be like going to a battle field; if so, you need to seek employment elsewhere. But, let's be real. Sometimes, we have to work with whatever hand we've been dealt and that can include a horrible boss, inept peers, a failing project, long work hours, etc., which can cause us to feel trapped.

There are some great places to work but if we buy into the bell curve theory: 15% of your coworkers are awesome, 15% are jerks, and the average 70% of employees by and large are decent with good and bad days. It's those 15% more or less who make working somewhere difficult. What's funny is that those people rarely leave. I tell decision-makers that people don't usually quit a job because of the work, but rather because of someone such as their boss. Unfortunately, in the workplace, some people are able to do more harm to you than their ability to help you. What do I mean by that? An administrative assistant cannot get you a promotion, but she can withhold information or messages that can sabotage you. Doing harm or even bad is so much easier than helping or doing good for some people; not all people, but some people. This is not a comfortable subject because I want to see the light in people, but if we are totally honest with each other here, people are people, regardless of their title or position. Think about the quote "One enemy can do more hurt than ten friends can do good," by Jonathan Swift. People often possess the ability to harm which can be as damaging as the good that people do. What this says to me is that we have to be vigilant about our well-being because we are always in a position to be vulnerable.

Sometimes stepping into the office will cause you to have to be on your toes. And, maybe this is coming from my most recent experiences. However, what has happened to me is not new. I have trusted others and gotten burned; not to the same extent, but still harmed (or, as Swift said, 'hurt') over the years. Who hasn't trusted and believed in others and then gotten stabbed in the back? But, that is par for the course. If you are in the game, you will get your toes stepped on, feelings hurt or experience any host of things that make you feel awful. Sometimes negativity is rampant, and negative people are plentiful in the workplace.

You may not know it, but there may even be someone somewhere who has said that you have harmed them, and you may not even realize it. Everyone perceives things differently, but the one constant that is irrefutable is that you must do the right thing as your spirit calls you to do. You'll know it is the right thing because there is a still, yet quiet voice inside each of us based on spirit. So, I write this chapter to talk about ways to be spiritually connected and balanced to deal with the day-to-day activities of life in the workplace.

I can give you suggestions on how to handle difficult people and deal with those people who are negative and disruptive in our career/life, but there are so many personalities and ways of being a jerk that addressing such would require a separate book. So, what I can do is share with you how to take care of yourself and protect yourself against those obstacles and/or energies that you can't always see but you definitely know are there. You cannot control or change people, but you can control and change how you will respond. In my opinion, the best way to fight negativity whether it is a negative day, person, situation, etc. is through spirituality. There are numerous things you can do to find balance, such as meditate, pray, practice mindfulness, exercise, walk, etc. All these methods are aimed at achieving one goal, which is to slow down and, eventually, completely stop the incessant activities in our minds. This will allow you to hear what you need to hear and see what you need to see to make your next move the best move, or no move at all. Spirituality is not a destination; it's a journey. It's experiencing the joys and pains with your whole self. You stumble, you fall, and you get back up to be better and do better in the next step.

There was this wonderfully insightful video that I received many years ago. I was struggling to complete a long and arduous application process for a program that would allow my company to compete for substantial government contracts. It was an awful process. It was a government program for minority set-asides. The application process was daunting based on it being intrusive, unfair, and the list goes on and on. I wanted to give up on the process, but my team kept pushing and encouraging me. As you read this story, keep in mind that the cross can be indicative of whatever you may rely on but may see as a burden, as well. Don't get wrapped around the religious symbolism. The video was of a little cartoon guy walking in what appeared to be a desert area in the heat. He was carrying a cross which was pretty long and heavy; similar to the application process. He would stop and wipe his forehead and continue to struggle carrying the cross. After what seemed like a long journey of sweating and struggling to carry that heavy cross, he finally asked God to remove the cross or lighten his load. He then asked for a saw, which he received, and commenced to cutting off the bottom portion of the cross. He was now delighted that the cross was more manageable and easy to carry. Slowly he felt the heaviness again, and requested another saw to cut off a little more length off of the cross. He was walking, whistling and carrying a lighter burden. Within time he started encountering people with their crosses, and everyone continued their journey. As they all walked, they came to a steep ravine that they all needed to cross to get to the other side. One by one, people started laying down their cross to create a bridge for themselves to get to the other side. Unfortunately, our friend with the shorter cross didn't have enough length to reach the other side. How often have we wanted less to get more? How often have we asked to be liberated from something that was actually for our highest and greatest good? He needed that entire cross for future valleys. The story is not about the cross but rather what you are going through or carrying that is preparing you for something else, especially when we find ourselves in the valley.

Here are a few techniques, exercises, activities, etc. to help you find solace when things seem to be piling up, work becomes overwhelming or you simply feel as if you have lost your way in this game. And, more importantly, these are practical ways to practice spirituality:

1. **Meditation**

    Some regard meditation as mental concentration on something. Others believe we meditate when we imagine something that gives us peace or satisfaction. I have some form of prayer and meditation daily! What are you doing to keep composure, have balance, and find peace and tranquility throughout your hectic day? Prayer is when I talk to God, and meditation is when I allow God to talk to me. Sometimes, we are so busy praying that God can't get a word in. There are days when the good fight is too difficult to bear, and we simply cannot imagine going on. That's when we must have a coming to the altar talk with ourselves. That talk with yourself is: what are you doing? Why are you doing it, and more importantly is it for your highest and greatest good? I will coach professionals who are miserable with an assignment. I ask them why they continue to do something that goes against every cell in their body and they just state that they have to so that they can get their ticket stamped. Sometimes the ticket that we believe we want stamped is taking us on the wrong path to a destination that we really don't want. The angst and pain that you feel is your spirit telling you to abort the mission. But you don't listen. That is when you become physically ill, start subconsciously sabotaging yourself, and doing things that you don't even understand. Why not save yourself from the stress and just listen to your higher self, your spirit, and let go of whatever you are holding onto in hopes of getting something you probably don't even want? So, I recommend that you meditate to go deep within to figure out what spirit is saying to you. Try to find meaning or rather a message in your mess. There are numerous ways to meditate. This is as personal as a pair of undergarments. You must find something that fits you. You can easily Google or YouTube meditating to see what techniques may work best for you.

2. Pray, and Don't Worry

In nearly every circumstance that seems to be beyond our control, you have an option. "Either you pray or worry; don't do both," said the great philosopher, Curtis Jackson a.k.a. 50 Cent, while being interviewed by Oprah Winfrey. I have found over the years that I would go into my prayer room that I had built in my house. I had altars, positive pictures, candles, oils and incense, music and other items that made me feel in touch with the universe. I would be in my prayer room in the morning before going to work, and back in there before I went to bed to rest my mind and to just say thank you. But, when the shit would hit the fan, I retreated to that room to pray. I would pray for myself, my company, my children, my family, my employees, and everyone whom I believed needed an intercessory prayer. I would sometimes pray aloud with tears streaming down my cheeks, hoping that God would hear my cry. And, then, I would extinguish the candles, turn off the music, leave the room and go someplace to worry. Yep, all that and then I would insult God by worrying. I basically asked for something and then basically told God that I doubt that he could do it or would do it. In either case, I worried as a way to deal with whatever was happening.

I remember that I used to have my students write down one thing that they were truly worried about or a problem, and then I would walk around the room with a trash can and ask them to ball up the paper and throw it in the trash. I would then sit the trash can by the door and ask if they would give me their undivided attention during class and pick up their problem on the way out. That may have seemed that I was making light of some real heavy problems that people were having but what could they really do with that problem within that hour just by thinking or worrying about it? I also would ask them to think of their problem. I would look at the clock and say to them, "Begin. Start thinking of your problem and pour all your energy into thinking about it, and let's see what happens." We all laughed after a minute of sitting there in silence, but that is what we often do. We think about something that we cannot change by worrying. Pray or worry? Sometimes I feel the need to do both, but it doesn't serve me well. So, I'm sticking with prayer coupled with meditation. Nearly every circumstance we encounter, inexplicably we have what we need. I needed that government status that was difficult to attain, based on the application process. I started earning multi-million dollar contracts for my company that I would otherwise not have been able to secure without that government program. I thank God that I didn't give up and that I suffered through the process. What if we occasionally take an inventory of things that cause difficulties to determine why they are there and to count it all as joy? This will allow you to accept your fate and worry less.

3. **Aromatherapy**

   When I say spirituality, people often think of religion, but by now, I hope you can see that spirituality is a practice. It is whatever allows you to have balance, tranquility and serenity, despite life's ups and downs. I often hear people say that they want to get home and crawl into the bed or that they can't even get out of bed when experiencing depression.

   There was one situation; wherein, a prominent pastor of a church reached out to me to discuss her severe depression that had kept her in bed for a couple of days and she had given people the excuse that she simply wasn't feeling well, which was the truth but not at the heart of the matter. After listening to her, I suggested that she get up and take a shower. I recommended that she take a shower and use a soap that had a fragrance different from what she was accustomed to. I have found that this can help a person move through negative feelings such as being tired, overwhelmed, depressed, worried, etc. Of course, it doesn't solve the problem, but aromatherapy soothes the spirit through the senses. There is something about smells and invigorating the senses that will allow you to feel better.

   I write about this because you may simply have a grueling day at work and need to release tension. Instead of making that stiff drink, pouring a glass of wine, watching a mindless television show or crawling into bed, take a bath or step in the shower and stimulate your senses. This is known as aromatherapy. According to Wikipedia, "Aromatherapy uses plant materials and aromatic plant oils, including essential oils, and other aromatic compounds for the purpose of altering one's mood, cognitive, psychological or physical well-being, in essence, spirit."

   There are two primary ways to introduce scents into your system: inhalation and absorption. Inhalation can be achieved while at your desk. You can rub essential oil(s) between your hands and cup your hands over your nose to breathe in the scent. This can be really effective in preparing for an encounter that may be filled with conflict or stress. You can place a scent on your hands and inhale it on your way to the meeting or while waiting for your turn to speak. In your home you, can use a diffuser or warmer. Then there is the bath; wherein, you can immerse yourself in the scent. The bath can also be used for absorption as you sit and soak for 20 minutes or more. Absorption can also be achieved by applying an essential oil directly to the skin or massaging it in for a length of time. I have found adding an essential oil to a scentless lotion as a wonderful start to my day.

Aromatherapy is a profitable industry. When we think of aromatherapy, we usually think of the holistic practitioner or spa professional. However, store shelves are filled with candles, oils and sprays for consumers who don't think of the products as alternative medicine but rather a way to make their environment soothing, refreshing or warm. I think on a subconscious level, people recognize the benefits and buy the products. There is a body, mind and spirit connection that you should not ignore. I am saying that stimulating your senses can improve your mental well-being. And, the great thing about aromatherapy is that it can be achieved and practiced anywhere. I challenge you to rub an essential oil on your hand and inhale before entering or exiting a stressful meeting. The list of uses is endless. If you would like to experience aromatherapy here are some scents and their purposes, according to www.aromatherapy.com:

- **Stress Relief**
  Bergamot, Chamomile, Lavender, Lemon, Orange, Patchouli, Vanilla, and Ylang Ylang

- **Anxiety/Fear**
  Bergamot, Chamomile (Roman), Cedarwood, Frankincense, Jasmine, Lavender, Neroli, Patchouli, Rose, and Sandalwood

- **Sadness/Grief**
  Bergamot, Chamomile (Roman), Clary Sage, Frankincense, Grapefruit, Jasmine, Lavender, Lemon, Orange, Rose, Sandalwood, and Ylang Ylang

- **Fatigue**
  Basil, Bergamot, Clary Sage, Frankincense, Ginger, Grapefruit, Jasmine, Lemon, Patchouli, Peppermint, Rosemary, and Sandalwood

- **Agitation**
  Chamomile (Roman), Lavender, Mandarin, and Sandalwood

4. **Living Your Purpose**

A quote is attributed to Mark Twain as saying, "The two most important days in your life are the day you are born and the day you find out why."

From the time I was a young woman to a few years ago, I would visit readers, also referred to as psychics. For the most part they were great in terms of sharing with me things about me and my journey, although a few times I've been scared to death from "fortunes" that were wrapped in bad news or even scams. At any rate, nearly every reputable reader has shared with me that I am on a mission that is aligned with spirituality. I've known all my life that I had been called to lead others, serve God and heal. It's pretty clear cut for me. Although, I haven't always been obedient to this calling, which I will talk about a little later. For now, I'm just laying a foundation that will allow me to spring board to areas that are difficult to reach without putting them into context.

A few years ago, I launched two new projects, i.e. Career Coffee Chats and writing for Inc. Magazine. The coffee chats were a weekly teleconference on Wednesdays from 10:00 am to 11:00 am; wherein, I invited my audience to call into my personal conference line. Listeners as far away as Hawaii and Washington, DC. called in. I spoke on topics that I believed impacted the call-in audience. The topics included mentoring, leadership, topics from my books (diversity, communications, thinking skills, playing the game, being a first generational success, etc.) and a host of hot items like likeability, dipping your pen in the company's inkwell, career mapping, networking, spirituality, and more. This complimentary professional development series allowed me to pour into others. This phrase is often unclear. Pour into others mean to give of myself. We all have something to give that is considered our gift. My gift is healing through words, listening and advising. When I do this: I'm pouring myself into someone. It's like a pitcher of energy and someone is the cup. The coffee chat idea was born out of recalling how I successfully built my company through relationships which centered on many coffee chats with clients and potential clients. Decision-makers had a very limited amount of time to meet with me, so I would offer to grab a cup of coffee with them, as my treat. I spent 75% of my time talking about the above topics as they pertained to them personally or their employees, while the remaining period of time was about delivering a product/service, i.e. sales. I learned early on in my career that people, especially leaders, often needed to have someone pour into them. Theodore Roosevelt is attributed as saying, "Nobody cares how much you know, until they know how much you care." That was my secret ingredient in a recipe for creating healthy and supportive client relationships I have come to accept that my gift is healing through words. I gather strength and momentum by healing others and I do that by pouring into them. I hope to die an empty vessel; wherein, I have poured all that I have into others. But the interesting thing is that I get refilled and refueled by pouring. That is what living your purpose does; it fuels you. I believe our purpose is what we are called to do, and everyone's purpose is different. But, the crux is being able to be rejuvenated by whatever it is that you do. Here's how you can know your purpose: while others would be drained by what you do, you actually pick up speed by whatever activity you were designed to do as your purpose and passion. That is the greatest truth and knowledge you can discover about yourself. What fuels you?

The next project that I was exceedingly elated about was to have a weekly article posted online for Inc. Magazine. That was exhilarating because I was able to talk and write about my passion, which is mental wellness. I loved writing the articles that required researching, interviewing and capturing personal experiences as a leader and business owner, but weekly? I became a little drained and anxious about writing a mental column every week. It was counterproductive to be anxious when I had to write about anxiety, so I abandoned the column after a year. I could have easily written a monthly column, but weekly was far too much. That was a tough project, but very insightful for me and my readers. That column led to blogging, which brought a significant amount of joy. I would write my blog almost like it was a diary. I would write with transparency and vulnerability which allowed me to purge. In short, I was healing myself by healing others which happened because I was aligned with my purpose. Figure out your purpose and move towards it. When you are doing what you've been designed to do, you will have an unspeakable inner peace. This is where I must recommend that you read the first book and complete the exercises on finding your passion.

5. **Live with Intentionality**

I advocate setting your intentions at the beginning of the year, although being intentional can start any time. I debunk the use of New Year's Resolutions and encourage people to try a few other things that have proven to be useful for me on my career journey. I believe that everyone can attain more of what they want by living an intention-filled life and by working an intention-filled career, marriage, relationship, parenthood, or whatever you are seeking to achieve! Looking back over the years, you must ask yourself, "How much was planned and how much just happened to or for you?"

During one of my Career Coffee Chats, a caller chimed in that she has lived by the premise of hope. If you have ever heard me speak, you will know what I think about hope. I shared with the listeners that hope is not a strategy. I asked her to simply use the SMART technique of setting her intentions. This technique is attributed to Peter Drucker's Management by Objectives concept that all graduate level business and management students study. Since, the 80s many people have used this concept for various purposes ranging from goal setting to time management. For this purpose, make sure that whatever you desire is SMART because we often wish for things that aren't so smart:

Specific

Ask or think about exactly what you want. The problem with many people is that they don't really truly know what they want and what that looks like. Start with the end in mind. Be specific about what you want. You don't have to be specific about how to achieve what you want but you do need to know what you want.

Measurable

Make sure that what you want can be quantified. How many or how much of something do you want to acquire?

Attainable

What you envision and seek to acquire must be achievable. If you say you want a promotion, but it clearly requires that you relocate, yet you are unwilling to move because you think that you can persuade them to let you telecommute, then that can derail your dreams from materializing or prolong the process. What do you really want, and does it align with what you are ultimately seeking to achieve?

Results

What action and steps do you need to take to make this thing happen? What does achieving what you want look like? Specifically, what are the results of you putting into action what you need to do? Do you need to network your way to the HR person who will be hiring? Do you need to get on an online app to meet your next love? Or, maybe you just need to have a crucial conversation with someone. Do things that will create results.

Time Driven

When is the start and completion time for something to happen? You can't leave things to chance and just hope that it happens. There is a time and season for all things and you need to set dates for your actions/steps and then keep a time table of whether you are hitting certain points at the right time or not to evaluate your progress.

SMART is merely the acronym to make sure you are on the right track. You have to manage your expectations which means being realistic, and at the same time putting your desires into action.

6. **Speaking Your Truth into Existence**

Many years ago, I would come up with one word that would drive my actions and thoughts, versus a New Year's Resolution. I would have words like love, patience, understanding, authenticity, courageous, etc. I recommend that you create a word to drive your actions. Each year, I think about things that I would like to modify in my behavior and I drill down to see what would cause that change.

As I shared with a group while speaking, 2014 was a kick-ass year and not in the most positive way. Little did I know that things were going to get worse. At that time, I needed to develop something that would carry me through and support my vision. That word was courage. I would sign off my emails with *Courageously*. I set my intentions and thoughts on being more courageous in every area of my life, which meant speaking my truth. The list was exhaustive in the many ways I wanted to live courageously. I was becoming courageous. I continued to grow in the area of courage because I had set that as my intention. So, I challenge you to think of a word that will drive your actions and to keep it always at the forefront of your mind as you go through your day. You will be amazed at what you will accomplish as you live up to that word. Go a step further and share your word(s) with others, which will ensure some level of accountability. When you tell people about your word(s), it places pressure on you to live it because you know people are now watching.

Now, if you came up with a word, you are now riding a bike with training wheels. Try this for a year: the same word. Don't change the word, but rather be consistent to see measurable results. I hope you practice your word and journal your results of living up to your word. Now, here's the next step: take off the training wheels and speak your truth. By this I mean, make a statement. For instance, my statement moved from courage to "Being Courageous to Live My Truth." I would place that at the end of my email messages and I used it in place of sincerely, respectfully, etc. It was my signature line. Some people would inquire, but overall it was a statement to the world that I was courageous and seeking to live my truth. That took courage in and of itself. Think of a phrase that will capture the essence of your journey and what you will accomplish as a result of that word. It is so liberating. Not to put words in your mouth but it can be sentences like: Allowing my light to shine, accepting change to move forward, helping others to help themselves, etc. You get the picture. It is basically your mission statement.

I recall an incident where I was writing a response to someone via email and when I got to the end of the message, I saw my statement, which I added into the stationary signature. What I wrote in the body of the email didn't align with my signature statement, "Being Courageous to Live My Truth." I was compelled to go back and rewrite that letter. Your phrase will hold you accountable to yourself. If you say that you will be patient to allow others room to grow, but you blast someone for a mistake, justly or not, you may have to step back and ask yourself, are you being patient and are you allowing people to grow before you send the message. I love this stuff. It's about changing our behavior and outlook on things. You must see that what you do and where you are can have an alternate pathway, if you rearrange your thoughts and how you see things. I think having a phrase that drives your behavior is like a pair of glasses with unique lenses that you created.

7. **Visualization**

   What was very helpful for me in creating change and manifesting more of what I wanted was visualization: seeing what I want. To do this I create a vision board. A vision board is a paper posted board that has pictures, words, symbols, etc. that describe what you want to bring into reality. If you see it, you can achieve it. I became such a master at creating vision boards that I started having New Year's Eve parties where people would come to my home and work on their vision board, and late in the evening we would share our board by presenting it to the group and explaining it. A vision board allows your creative juices to flow by creating a map for both your conscious and subconscious mind to follow.

   A vision board is merely a tool to visualize your intentions and manifest your desires. I recommend that you buy a poster board and gather a variety of magazines or images from the Internet. You can then cut and paste pictures, words and symbols. For instance, if you want more financial freedom, you may cut out a picture of people traveling, dollar signs, the word investment, wealth, etc. and so forth. I think that you should write down a list of what you desire and begin searching for those items that you can place on your board. Interestingly, you will find that your higher self will add things to your list that you consciously didn't think of initially. Cut out the shapes and paste them onto a board with no particular pattern. It is your board. You may want to section off areas or make a collage. I'm pretty organized and orderly, so I create more of a story or flow with my pictures and I use glitter and stuff to make it look pretty. Just allow yourself to let go and let things flow to you, and you will have this beautiful work of art when you are finished. When my guests would be in a room devoted to creating their vision board, there was so much synergy and positive energy flowing. People started sharing pictures with one another as they began to tell each other what they needed. It was like being a kid again and making a list for Santa. Now, take the board and place it somewhere conspicuous so that you will see it often or at some point through the day (preferably morning). You will focus your attention and energy on what is on the board, and you'll be amazed at what you will start to manifest. I've created vision boards for many years. They work for me, and they can work for you, too.

8. **Music: A Language for the Soul**

    Have you ever noticed the music that is played in the grocery stores, elevators, dental offices, and other places you frequent? What do these merchants know that maybe many people don't? Aside from the marketing value associated with playing some great Steely Dan to cause you to put items in your basket that you don't even need, there is another role that music plays. It can alter your mood. Research has shown that music can be a natural anti-depressant.

In an article in the *Journal of Positive Psychology*, it is suggested that passively listening to music as a potentially powerful tool will enhance one's emotional well-being. Music can have a profound effect on improving your workspace and your mental well-being during the 9 to 5 workday. However, you often find professionals working at their desks in silence or playing music that actually has an adverse effect on their psyche; thus, their spirit when we consider the mind, body and spirit connection.

Music therapy has been used for centuries as a way to restore energy, improve mood, and even help the body heal more naturally. Soothing tunes foster the release of serotonin, a hormone that fosters happiness and a general sense of well-being. It also flushes the body with dopamine, a neurotransmitter that makes you feel good. Music also paves the way for the release of norepinephrine, a hormone that brings about euphoria and elation. Who can deny that we all need a little extra something to get us through the day and to remain balanced emotionally? Let's face it: professionals have moments of anxiety when dealing with the budget, unreasonable clients, or employee issues.

Calming background music can significantly decrease irritability and promote calmness. Knowing that certain kinds of music can alleviate stress is one thing; being mindful in choosing what kind of music to listen to is another. Choose your music as carefully as you choose what you are going to wear on a first date (TMI about me).

Check the pulse on how you are feeling. Become aware of your feelings and then play music that will put you in a better place. Oddly enough, I have on my iPod playlist a category titled "melancholy." People are drawn to depressing music when they are depressed. Now that I know that such music doesn't serve me well, I listen to music that is described as Warm Feelings, Power, Energy, etc. I do this by paying attention to my mood. You can find on YouTube various music entitled meditation, jazz, relaxation, etc. that will lift your spirits.

Spirituality as a Viable Option

I want to close this chapter with one more personal story or testimony. I work with leaders who often carry the weight of the company on their shoulders. If this resonates with you, put into practice the things that will create an impact immediately and then slowly infuse other techniques over time. Reportedly, Winston Churchill said, "You can always count on Americans to do the right thing - after they've tried everything else." I thought the quote was funny, although unfortunately true. This can be said about people in general. Sometimes, we try everything long before we try spirituality. I'm not talking about religion. I'm talking about trusting in your faith in whatever you believe.

Several years ago, something unheard of happened! The US Federal Government shut down. I started my company as a result of being hired to help federal employees transition out of the Federal Government in 1995. It was unheard of that the US Federal Government would ever lay off workers, but I was hired to offer transitional assistance for something that never took place. It was

Chapter 5: The Practicality of Spirituality

2013 or so and I was right back where I started, but in a much more vulnerable place. Eighteen years prior, all I had to concern myself with was myself. In 2013, I had to be concerned with employees, their livelihood and their families. I couldn't afford a government shutdown, but that was exactly what happened. My client, the US Federal Government, closed its doors and sent everyone home, except those in critical capacities such as the military (sigh).

I went home early on the eve of the shutdown. I was glued to the television as I watched CNN give blow-by-blow details on how the American government was shutting down. My youngest son came home and asked me why I was at home because he has never known me to be home before him. I walked over to him and said, "The government is shutting down," as a tear welled up in my eye. I could tell that he had no idea what I was talking about at his young and innocent age. I decided right then and there that I would not worry him by placing an adult issue on his mind. I told him to do his homework so that we could go out for pizza. I slumped back on the couch and continued watching CNN in hopes of hearing something that would sound like hope.

Every news station reported on the impending shut down and commenced a countdown by displaying a clock in the corner of the screen to show how much time the government had to approve their budget. I sat there for another hour, and something came across me that gave me hope. I couldn't find hope on television which is the last place I would have expected to hear anything positive, anyway, right? Instead my soul said, "God is still working. God hasn't shut down." That gave me a moment of peace, and I turned off the television to ignore the inevitable. There was nothing that I could do to change what was happening, but I could change how I would handle the situation. I decided to trust in God and spend time with my son. When you are faced with difficulties don't abandon your beliefs.

A lesson from all this is that what took years to unravel can be mended in moments. I felt that I lost nearly everything of value i.e. my home, my business, my money, material things too numerous to mention and even my way. But, I categorically learned that I gained everything of value. I look at my brother whose life was turned inside out and within a few years he was featured in a Hollywood movie based on his downfall. On a spiritual level, things can turn around in such a way that what you gain is far greater than what you lost. The pains you experience are merely temporary. I can't tell you how many times I kept thinking that I was living a nightmare. I am fortunate because most of my life has been better than what I deserved. A side note about getting better than what I deserve: when toasting before sipping a drink, I will now say, "May I get whatever I deserve, and may you get what you deserve." Immediately, an uncomfortable smile will come across people's face. I then explain by describing what the world would be like if we all got what we deserved. That's when people admit that there would be less crime, more thoughtfulness, etc. I love it.

It's been a wonderful dream at times. Then that dream became a nightmare. When your dreams become a nightmare it's time to wake up. I'm completely awake now. There have been times when I wished that I could go to sleep and wake up in the future when everything has been resolved. But that's not living. In short, that is a coma and I certainly don't want that. I just wanted the pain to end, the confusion to go away and justice to be served in the embezzlement case. I couldn't wait for an outside force to make it happen, because I felt that most of it was out of my control. And, that is where spirituality comes in. I had to stop fretting and start believing that everything works out for my highest and greatest good, especially when I am living a purpose-filled life that is in Divine order. I needed to practice my spirituality more than ever to find a space where I could experience tranquility, serenity and peace despite all that was happening; and, that is what spirituality is truly all about for me. Lastly, you don't call on spirituality when things are going wrong, rather, it is a day-to-day practice. The more you practice spirituality, the more you are able to handle misfortunes with grace and receive blessings with gratitude. I end this chapter with this prayer that you can use at any time for any situation and for true practicality of spirituality. You don't have to use the word Lord. You can replace it with your name or whatever you consider your source:

> "Lord, grant me the strength to accept the things I cannot change, the courage to change the things I can, and the wisdom to know the difference."

Reinhold Niebuhr

Chapter 6

Indigoisms for Insight

Over the years, I have played the game by both common and uncommon unwritten rules, and there are some rules that I have added that have supported my success. Here is what I think: this is what I know are general truths I've learned and practiced along the way. For instance, I'm over in Asia, right? Dating has been very interesting, to say the least. I have considered men who I ordinarily wouldn't give a second glance if I were back in the US. Okay, this may be TMI (too much information), but hear me out. I took a step back and decided that I need to go with what works for me, even if that means being alone or having fewer dates than I'm accustomed to, right? So, just the other day, I said to myself that my personal motto going forward will be, 'I'm settled in but not settling,' which is now an Indigoism. It means that I'm comfortable with where I live and who I am (settled), but I'm not going to date just anyone because the pickings are slim here (settling). It's these types of things that I have picked up or rather made up along the way both personally and professionally that have brought meaning to my journey.

So, this chapter is about things that I've discovered along the way, for which I have coined the name: Indigoisms. Here is what I think: there are many paths you will take on your journey. This is is what I know: you must find your true north. I believe what has served me well is that "I expect but don't accept', which is another Indigoism. For instance, I expect that dating will be somewhat of a challenge for a myriad of reasons, but I don't accept that I have to be disingenuous or someone that I am not. I expect that I will need to continue to play the game, even at my age, my status and my experience, but I don't accept when professionals ask unreasonable things of me to satisfy their own ego.

In this chapter, I am sharing with you some insights on what helped me on my journey to finding my voice, being authentic and removing barriers to success. My career has been a fantabulous (fantastic/fabulous) journey. It has more climbs and heights than drops and valleys; although, the drops were significant. I say to you, don't be afraid to take risks, to trust people and see the good in people. You'll encounter some haters and even Decepticons like the Transformer machines, but if you apply the bell curve theory, 15% of your encounters will be with people who want to see you succeed and will throw you their support in whatever way they can, whether it is to bring you coffee on their coffee run, or pitching you for a position in their company. Then 15% of the people you meet will be haters. Some will be open about their disdain for you, while some will act as if they are in your corner. Then there are those in the middle, i.e. the bulk or majority of people. They can take you or leave you, they may be indifferent, and/or are neutral until you give them a reason to move to one side or the other on the curve.

Just as I would tell a manager developing her employees, remove the bottom feeders, i.e. haters. Those are people who can do more harm than good. Don't expend your limited amount of resources and time on them. The return will not be worth the investment. And, don't ignore your adorers. They don't need a lot of time, but you do need to let them know that they are valued. Communicate with them to keep them abreast of your activities and show appreciation by supporting them. But, the bulk of your time is moving people from the middle to the top. Share with them your resources to help them grow; grab coffee and get to know each other better, invite them to things, and show up to events to support them. In short, figure out how to be what they need you to be, while still being authentic. For example, I love volunteering for things that align with my values. If there is someone in the middle and I want them on the right side, I will ask if I can accompany them on a visit to a local shelter where they sit on the board or donate their time or do something that supports their interests.

Many moons ago, I did that with a guy who was a leader in a company that I wanted to have as a client. His time was limited so I could never get an appointment to meet with him. I did a little research and found out that he sat on boards. As a volunteer with a nonprofit where he was on the board, he delivered meals on the weekend to people infected with AIDS. I contacted him and asked if I could accompany him to deliver meals one Saturday morning. As we drove around the city delivering meals, he explained his passion for the organization which was Project Open Hands. I then asked him if I could take one of the meals to the person listed on his route. We pulled up to a house and he handed me the meal and told me that it was for someone named Mary. I walked up to the house and there was a little girl about six years old and a boy around the same age sitting on the steps. I asked the little girl if her mom was home. She told me that her mommy wasn't home. Then I looked at the name again and asked if Mary was home. She said, "That's me!" That meal was for her: she was Mary and she had AIDS. I gave her the box of food in utter shock. She took the meal that she was waiting for and sat down on the steps and began to eat happily sharing what she had with the little boy. I could barely make it to the car before shedding tears. I signed up to deliver meals on my own route. I would include my entire family on this weekly weekend activity. Years later, I even launched a satellite branch in a neighboring city based on my commitment to the cause, and I became a board member. That guy and I became great friends even though I never won a contract with his company. But, I received far more than a possible contract, I received the opportunity to touch lives.

If you ever feel that doing things to get things is about using people, then think again. Get rid of that stinky thinking. This is networking at its greatest level. I've had people approach me for no other reason than for me to help them. I don't take offense or mind. People will always want something for some reason or another. Let's not be naïve. I think it's about how we do it that makes the difference. I've seen people manipulate in ways that are as trifling as withholding bits and pieces of information to a full-fledged hiding of information. Be clear that you are up front with people on why you want to meet, network, etc., which helps you minimize the chances of being seen as manipulating or using them. I think that when I let someone know my desires and give them a chance to make an informed decision on whether to meet with me or help me, I've done my part and now the ball is in their corner to accept or reject my offer, suggestions, invitation, etc. I use persuasion versus manipulation. I've never met anyone who said, "Yes, you're Dr. Indigo. I gotta be careful with you. I hear that you trick people into liking you, supporting you and being your friend." I'm careful to manage relationships and expectations. So, manage the pool of people already in your circle and work towards strengthening those relationships. Acquire the ability to move contacts from meaningless to meaningful. It will be an impactful differentiator in your life and career. Your net worth is measured by your network. Can you contact people to garner support directly or indirectly? It's not about money any longer for me, but rather who I have access to and who is willing to have a reciprocal relationship with me. This is what I know.

I'm not going to downplay all the other stuff like intellect, skills, experience, etc. But, here is what I know: when you have nothing, you better have personality. In short, you need the likeability factor. Sure, I have a Ph.D., which represents intellect, by and large. But, when I moved to Asia, I was ignorant of the cultures, customs, etc. which was an obstacle in some ways; and then there were the hurdles of not knowing anyone. But, I was likeable which caused a few people to support me. And, my son Sinclair who served as the company's business developer was likeable, which also opened doors for us. This led to being invited to functions and other activities that helped us to gain exposure. It wasn't our degrees per se, but rather the degree to which people accepted us, i.e. liked us.

Allow me to digress for a moment to set the tone for the next few pages. This book has been in my heart for many years. There just hasn't been an appropriate time to write, until now. There are both common and uncommon unwritten rules, and here are some things that I have learned along the way that I believe served me well. I would like to share them with you. Some things I intuitively knew, while other things I heard said by other people. I will attempt to attribute whatever was gleaned from others when possible, but some things I have practiced for so long that I can't recall where it came from, yeah. I've also mixed some of the unwritten rules for success with what I have termed as "Indigoisms". I find that during speaking engagements there are go-to expressions that I use, and they have helped me and countless others. Take what works for you, share with others and tuck away what doesn't work for now, but might at some point. These are not in order of importance, but I encourage you to take each and figure out how it applies to you and your circumstance. This is what I know:

1. **Get Your Rest**

    Whenever, I speak to friends or colleagues I care about, I always say to them, "Get your rest." Getting the proper amount of sleep is critical to playing the game and managing your career. Before a game, professional football teams in America check into a hotel so that the men could get their sleep and rest, at least that was the practice at one time. I heard Iyanla Vanzant say something like this, "You need to go to sleep on the same day that you wake up." In short, if you wake up at 7:00 am on Wednesday, you need to be back in bed and on your way to sleep by 11:59 pm on Wednesday. Some people constantly wake up in the morning and go to bed at 1:00 am, which is the next morning. That's another day, which is fine on the weekend, but during the work week? Tsk tsk tsk. Your body needs the rest to reset and recover. There should be a number that we can call to report our neighbors when we see their lights on every night until 2:00 am during the work week, knowing they have to get up in a few hours for work. That's abuse and neglect of oneself (then again, let me take my nosey butt to sleep).

2. **Connect to Connect**

   Allow yourself to be available and open to connect or to have casual encounters. People often shut themselves off from each other, especially strangers. But, that is where you may find the right piece to complete the puzzle you've been working on. Just the other day, I was chatting with this guy when he began sharing with me that he is passionate about hospitality. After explaining what he wants to ultimately do with his career, I got excited because I shared with him that I wanted a glamping (glamorous camping) business on the island where he lives. There was instant synergy as I shared my dreams and he shared his goals. This is what I call the Reese's Effect. This is where a great chocolate candy was discovered by blending chocolate with peanut butter which is now the Reese's Peanut Butter Cups. We would not have known about this potential opportunity if we did not connect. Then a few weeks ago, I met a guy who owns a beach resort on a different island. I can easily see introducing the two of them. I not only connect on a higher level knowing that what I need will be sent my way, but I connect others knowing that I can be a blessing to others. You may miss receiving what you need if you rely solely on people already in your network. Connect and then connect.

3. **Get People Out of Your Head**

   I read this quote back in the 90s, "You can't beat an enemy who has an outpost in your head," I Googled it and there is a slightly different version attributed to a woman who wrote a book in 2013. So, I will not reference her because I know it was a guy who said it first. But, the point is to stop thinking about others and just focus on yourself. When you find yourself trying to anticipate what someone else is going to do, versus playing your game your way, this will cause you to have to play harder and maybe without much success. At least, that is how I interpreted it. It may mean something totally different to someone else. It can also mean to not let people, especially foes, get into your head by listening to their comments that might discourage you, etc. Then, last but not least, it could mean telling the wrong people too much; whereby, they use your words and information against you because they know what you are thinking.

4. **Grow by Listening**

   Why is this so hard? We have two ears to hear and one mouth to talk, but we act as if we have two mouths and one ear. You can find out more about what a person wants by listening, and you can find out a lot about yourself by listening. You see, when you listen, you are quiet, which allows you to process. In your processing you may discover that something bothers or excites you, which can lead to discovering things about yourself. Growth doesn't come from talking as much as it comes from listening.

5. **Quality and Integrity are the Best Advertisements**

    Nothing is wrong with speaking up for yourself and what you do, but if you and your work are outstanding that will speak for itself. Even when something is small and insignificant, do your best. Those seem to be the things that impress people the most. People expect you to do your best for high profile and important things, but *wow* people with the small stuff and see how that will create more opportunities for you. When I was in graduate school, I had a professor who was legally blind. He could see things but with much difficulty. When I submitted my papers, I would type using a ridiculously large font. I would also use very large fonts for slides. During a ride home, a friend was teasing me about playing up to the professor. At the time, that wasn't my intent: I was naturally playing the game and didn't know it. What was in my heart and mind were to make life easier for this instructor by giving him requested papers that he could easily read. In my opinion, he deserved (there's that word again) that level of respect and support. When I received my paper after he graded it, I was so pleased because he wrote 'W O W' across my paper. He also wrote something to the effect that no one had ever taken his disability into consideration, etc. etc. etc. Did I get an A? Of course, that is a part of playing the game to win.

    As a side note, let integrity be a common thread in all that you do, sprinkled with a little consideration. People appreciate people who are considerate. However, the crux of this point is that people will come to trust you based on your integrity. I've come to appreciate the reputation I've built by having integrity. People have done things on my behalf with just a handshake because I have demonstrated that I am true to my word and that I always seek win win situations.

6. **I Only Want Happy Money**

    I have learned along the way that all money is not good money. For instance, you accept a job with a crazy travel schedule. Yes, you'll get a raise, but you won't see your children which is what you say that you value. Maybe that new position is not right for you and within time what seems like happy money will become unhappy money. For me as a business owner, it means to do business with clients whom I like, trust and value. Whenever I do something for sheer money, it doesn't really work to my advantage because I'm usually not happy as I chase down payments, have to do work that I don't like doing, or work with people whom I wouldn't sit next to on the bus. It is my goal and desire to have happy money: money that I enjoy earning. If you want more joy in your career; don't chase the money, chase the joy. Lastly, I tell potential clients the same. I don't want you to hire me if what you are going to pay me is going to make you unhappy, and I don't want to take the contract if what I'm being paid is going to make me unhappy. Neither of us will be happy which will be a source of contention.

7. You Can't Get to Heaven by Putting Other People through Hell

This is something which I try to be mindful of. You've heard me say this throughout the book. You don't have to hurt, embarrass, cheat, or do anything that will harm others to get to where you want to go. If you do, then shame on you! When you see that what you are doing is causing distress, stop and figure out another way (unless hurting people is your profession). There are many paths to where you want to go. The best is probably the road less travelled, as a book with that title indicates. But, I assure you that making other people feel miserable for your gain and quest is awful.

8. Rejection is Often Protection

Oh my God…thank goodness that we don't always get what we want. Sometimes we try so hard to get that perfect guy who we find out later isn't so perfect; or we hope for that fantastic job with a company that without warning goes out of business. Some things we just can't anticipate, right? But, what I love is that what we want doesn't always happen for us. Then we find out that it ends up being for our highest and greatest good. The message is to not mope and feel slighted when you don't acquire what you want because that rejection may be protecting you from something unbeknownst to you. Count it all as joy and keep it moving so that the right thing will arrive at the right time.

9. Let It be Easy

Sometimes, life can be hard, but it doesn't have to be. Let it be easy. That is what I love about Asia. It is easy living. People aren't as uptight, stressed out and angry as people in America. I've become less stressed and I'm learning to go with the flow a little more, and I like it. In fact, anytime I've had issues, raised my voice or had drama, I caused it. Yes, sometimes there is a lack of urgency and stuff from the locals, but my reactions are totally on me. They aren't yelling and clowning. It's me! I'm the common denominator. So, I had to change me and now things are much easier. I'm letting it be easy. I'm approaching more things with humility, humbleness and appreciation of others. Life is good. Now, that is a quote that should go on a T-shirt (wink).

10. You Get More of What You Focus On!

If you are focused on how hard things are or how unfair things are, you will attract more things that are hard and unfair. It's elementary, my dear. Focus on what is good and what makes you happy to attract more of that. "And, when you want something, all the universe conspires in helping you to achieve it," says Paulo Coelho. That is just one of the many laws of spirituality to which I ascribe.

11. Wherever You are, Get Everything You Can; and, Wherever You are, Give Everything You Got

This is something that I try to get employers to understand. They need to give to get. But, for you the reader, give everything you've got and get everything you can. It's a fair trade. You'll grow and develop, while the organization benefits in such a way that you may create a new position for yourself. I told the story in the last book about how I gave the least amount of effort to passing a physical test while in boot camp for the US Marine Corp. I thought that I could act as if I improved over time with little to no effort by barely passing the initial test. In short, I could give minimal effort throughout boot camp. What I didn't know was that the Drill Instructor (DI) had my records and knew that I was a record-holding cross-country runner, though I ran just enough to pass, right? Well, I was severely disciplined; thus, I never made that mistake again. The pendulum swung to the far side for me such that I now give more than 100% to everything. It has paid off for me time and time again.

12. Change is Like Planting a Seed

The things that we do such as activities, thoughts, etc. are seeds. When you plant a seed, you don't get the fruit the very next day. There are natural laws to everything. Allow time to work for you. Just because you do not see results quickly doesn't mean what you are doing isn't working. Whatever seeds you are planting will grow; just maybe not as fast as you would like.

Also, what you plant you will harvest; good and bad. This has never been more real to me than now. Here in Asia I have been embraced, supported and loved up by people of all walks of life. I'm overwhelmed with the love I have received from strangers and people who I recently met. Occasionally, I stay with a new friend in her wonderful beautiful home that could be in the *Better Homes and Gardens* magazine. She will not accept anything from me when I come to town for business. Then a colleague developed my marketing materials for a Women's Forum that I was offering. She felt that what I produced could be improved and she was right. There is a marketing specialist who is helping me recreate my brand. I don't have the money, but she asked me to simply pay her when I can. What? Who does that? I do that. And, that is what I am reaping. I have done absolutely nothing here to be so fortunate, but I planted seeds for many years back in the US and those plants are sprouting up like bamboo trees over here.

13. Plant Yourself Where You Can Grow

What may be considered a weed to some are wild flowers to others. Make sure you are planted where you are appreciated and where you can and will grow. Not all seeds will mature in all environments. When I came to Asia, I struggled and struggled. I was getting help and support here and there, but things weren't coming effortlessly or fast enough, in my opinion. I shared my story with this Chinese man who showed me some bamboo trees. He said to me that I was the bamboo. He also said that bamboo grows slowly in foreign or hostile soil. I felt that I was having a *Kung Fu* moment based on the 70s show that should have featured Bruce Lee but starred David Carradine. Supposedly, the bamboo takes about three years to get established. Once established, the new shoots that emerge in the spring (they will still only grow for 60 days) will continue to get bigger and more numerous from year to year as the colony grows towards maturity. Once, it emerges it will shoot up quickly to great heights, and it will be so strong and sturdy that it is unbreakable. His analogy hit home, and it encouraged me to hang in here. I am in the right place at the right time, and coincidentally, I'm going into my third year in Asia. I totally embrace the analogy: I believe it, receive it and will run with it. Are you where you want and need to be? Remove all the excuses and buts. I hear people tell me what they want to do and then they add but to their statement. They will say things like…, but I'm too old, …but, I don't have a degree, …but, my (you fill in the blank) will not understand. Honey, get your but(t) out of the way.

14. Understand Uncertainty to Know Certainty

Have you ever been in a situation where you just didn't know what you wanted? It is natural to experience this when seeking to leave a job for something else, when dating, when considering a new career, etc. I have found it useful to work backwards on things. In simplistic terms, you may not know what you want, but at least know what you don't want. There will be opportunities that will come your way and sometimes you will agree to things that you may not necessarily want because you didn't know what you wanted or, just as importantly, didn't want. If you are not clear on what you want because you don't know what all is available, at least know what you do not want. Let's take your career progression. You aren't sure about what you ultimately want to do or where you want to be, but at a minimum know what you don't want. For example, you should know that you don't want to work on a certain team or in a specific department, right? Or, you know that you hate presentations and sales. Knowing something is a good start for avoiding missteps. Well, don't take assignments that will lead you in the direction of the very thing you don't want. Think seriously about taking an opportunity that requires moving through a certain department or the natural progression is having a percentage of something you loathe included in the package at some point.

For example, in dating, you have your ideal person in mind, in terms of what characteristics and traits you would like in a partner. What will cause much unrest is to attract a person who has things about him/her that you don't like as well. Spend time exploring what will not work for you to recognize it and avoid it when it comes your way. The same things should be happening in your career. If you aren't clear on how to do this, or how to discover what you don't like, I recommend that you read the first book which is about career management. You need to spend time understanding your strengths, skills, abilities, etc., while exploring those things that are your weaknesses which are usually things you should avoid. Another book which I believe is helpful in this area is *StrengthsFinder 2.0* by Tom Rath.

15. Think About What Will Go Right Versus What Will Go Wrong

There is something to be said and valued in looking at the pros and cons of things. But, some people spend way too much time considering what will not work, or rather the downside of something versus what will go right. This limits your openness to take risks. There are greater rewards for higher risks. The worst fruit is on the ground where it has already ripened and fallen from the tree; then the low hanging fruit is fine but accessible to all; however, the fruit that is high up and out of reach is the prime produce. But, people will consider whether they might fall because the limb is less sturdy, they may be unable to reach it after much effort, and the list goes on and on for people not going after the better fruit. Those are the people who will settle for less, while you should focus not only on your being able to go out on a limb to get what you want, but also on what you will be able to do with all the fruit that you are going to get which is there for the taking. Shift your thinking to what will go right as opposed to what will not work. My son Sinclair is so good with that and I'm thankful that it has been contagious.

16. Career Development is for Career Management

You should be looking two years ahead for your next job or career move. I say two years because every job description basically requires two years of demonstrable experience. Allow time to work for you. Spend time looking across your organization to see what jobs exist and which are of interest to you. Start developing the knowledge, skills and abilities for that position which is how you will manage your career to new opportunities. You should complete an Individual Development Plan (IDP) which will include the mentors you need along the way, identify advocates who can sponsor you, shadow, volunteer, etc. so that when that job becomes available you are legitimately qualified. This is where I recommend that you re-read my first book.

17. If Your Company Doesn't Have Your Dream Job, Create It for Them and Yourself

Sometimes an organization doesn't know what it doesn't know. If you have read that xyz is where the industry is moving, and you believe that your company should consider adopting such, then pitch to leadership your research and how you can work on creating that position or role. Now, this is a risk because you can get stuck doing it as a part of your job without compensation, or they can hire someone else after you created it, which would suck. I'm not going to lie to you, it happens. But, instead of thinking of what can go wrong, let's focus on what will go well. If you successfully bring whatever they need into the organization, you may become invaluable; whereby, that could lead to managing/leading that program/project/role. And, you have just acquired a new ability, etc. to place on your resume. You can now demonstrate how you analyzed and researched to discover an innovative xyz that you launched in your company. I know that it works! I did it at a company. Everyone called me crazy because I basically did two jobs for several months. However, the skills and experience that I gained from that endeavor paved a way to entrepreneurship.

18. Give Yourself Permission to Want More

What is it that you really want, versus what is it that you and others have told you that you either deserve or can have? If you are not where you want and need to be, it may not be what is keeping you from the top; it may be who, and the who may be you. I have said this all around the world for many years and it still rings true. We limit ourselves. I'm amazed at how many people wait to be tapped on the shoulder for an opportunity. If you see what you want, ask for it. Take the initiative, but before you can take the initiative you must want it. Give yourself permission to want it despite whatever someone has said to you as a child/young adult, regardless of what hasn't worked in the past, etc. This is not solely about work. I was talking to someone and I mentioned something about happiness. He responded, "Doesn't everyone want to be happy?" I said, "No. I think that a lot of people are afraid to allow themselves to do or have things that will make them happy because of the possible fear of loss." Later that day, we were hanging out and I asked him if he wanted something, and he replied that he did, but he would pass. I looked at him and reminded him of our earlier conversation, and ended the discussion by saying, "Treat yourself: don't cheat yourself, baby." How often have you wished that you would have done something, but you didn't for whatever reason, and you regretted that decision? If you want to live with less regret, do more of what brings you bliss.

19. Never Say Yes When You Mean No and Vice Versa

Someone asked me how I kept my youthfulness, and I said that I never say yes when I mean no and I never say no when I mean yes. I don't play games with myself to appease self-limitations or to live up to someone's expectations of me. If I want to do something, I will do it. I have learned to live with less regrets. I had a girlfriend invite me to an evening out on the town; whereby, we would have dinner and I'd be her guest to see Beyoncé with a small group of women whom I didn't know. I thanked her, but I declined. She went on to say that she had back stage passes as if that would sweeten the pot. I explained to her that I'm not a girl's group kinda girl, I'm not into that kind of music, and I know that I wouldn't enjoy myself. Some things, you just know about yourself based on years of understanding (YOU). If I had said yes to that invite, I would have been miserable based on the type of music and concerts that I do enjoy. At the time, I could barely name one or two of her songs. Lastly, I know that I'm an outlier. I appreciate that my quirkiness can be peculiar to people who don't know me, especially among some women who can be less accepting of other women who are outliers. Trust me: I know what I know. That would have been a long night. But, the point is that I never say yes when I mean no. Some people may not like it, but this is where I must be true to myself, especially, when it doesn't impact my career. I have to do far too many things from 9 am to 5 pm that I may prefer not to do, so after 5 pm, when deciding what I will do with my free time, I choose to do me. So, I don't say yes when I mean no and don't say no when I mean yes.

20. Stop Listening to Random Voices in Your Head and Start Talking to Yourself

Sometimes, we hear that voice that sounds a lot like people who have discouraged us in one way or another. Stop listening to that voice and start talking to yourself. This means you have to start having meaningful conversations with yourself. Start telling yourself the things you want and need to hear. Treat yourself as if you are your best friend. If your friend wanted to apply for a new job, would you tell your friend that she will never get that job and that she isn't good enough? Heck no! You would tell that friend something like this, "Girl, I've been wondering why it was taking you so long. You deserve that job! You are the best thing that happened to that company. I got your back." Well, say those same things to yourself. Encourage, support and promote yourself through positive self-talk, even if you don't believe it, just yet. Be the friend you deserve and the friend that you are to others.

21. You May be Able to Forgive, but for Forgiveness You Must be Able to Ask

Yes, there is an entire chapter on this, but I can't emphasize enough that we must have the humility, compassion and courage to ask for forgiveness. I have a son who refuses to say that he is sorry. For some reason, it is as if he is admitting guilt or something. I have no idea why he is adamant about not saying he's sorry. Forgiveness is basically a word that aligns with sorry. It is not about guilt or blame, but the willingness to accept that what happened caused harm in some way whether it's your fault or not, intentional or unintentional. Maybe you feel as if you did not do the offense, but can you empathize that what happened caused someone to feel something other than good? Maybe you aren't sorry about what you did but can you be sorry for how that person feels? If you can't wrap your head around this, please reread the forgiveness chapter because you aren't getting it. This could prove to be the most powerful skill you possess as you enter new levels of success.

22. Help Those Who Deserve Your Help

If you recall, I mentioned in "Uncommon Unwritten Rules" that my biggest regret is when I did good things for the wrong people. You must develop discernment on how you will give of yourself and what you will give. But, more importantly, make sure that what you are giving is what someone wants. In addition, never give more than you can afford, that can mean mentally, physically, financially, etc. Some things that you give may knock the wind out of you. I told the story of how someone took advantage of my kindness, which I felt was horrible because I was trying to help that person. But, as she reminded me, she didn't ask for my help. You must really think about why you pour into others and give of yourself when it is not asked of you, and then you must be willing to not expect anything in return. If the person doesn't seek your help, but you offer it, then let that be your just reward. What you believe is helping someone may not be help in someone else's opinion. Also, try asking the person whether they want your help before doing things, based on what you believe a person will value or want. What I have found is that when we have expectations of people based on what we do for them, then our expectations are really premeditated resentment, yeah.

23. If I Take Good Care of People and Do Right, Life Will Take Good Care of Me and Do Right by Me

Sometimes you will not see your virtuous deeds rewarded but know for certain that everything comes back in one form or another. When I went through my storm, there were always life rafts and light houses to guide me. That was life taking care of me. The outpouring of love that I received in Asia was life taking care of me. As I grew my business in the US, it was my ability to care for my clients, employees and others that made the difference. I can look back over many negative incidents and see the positive blessings doubled to counteract all life's drops and falls, and I attribute that to my life's passion of taking good care of people.

24. Everything I Do is a Statement of What I Think I'm Worth

When I first arrived in Asia, I gave away books that I needed to sell, and I did a lot of presentations for free. Now granted, many conferences do not pay speakers and, in fact, request payment from the speaker, here in Asia. That's utter hogwash. Speaking for free ran counter to how I built my business in the US. I'm a professional speaker, so I must be paid. That's my livelihood. Also, I believe that free work begets free work and that people do not value what is not acquired through a value exchange. But, I gave away my talent and even books as I told myself that it was to rebuild. But maybe, just maybe, deep down I felt broken and not worthy of the fees that I would ordinarily charge when in the US, based on falling, which felt like failing. As I climbed my way out of the pit of pity, I regained my confidence and started requiring people to pay for my intellect, service, talent. etc. That was a statement of my worth. It was less about what people thought of me, but what I thought of myself. This could mean the work that you turn in, the projects you accept, the person you date, the friends you hang out with, and the list goes on. Determine your worth and align it to that which mirrors and demonstrates that worth.

25. Speak Your Truth

Everything doesn't need to be overlooked and everyone doesn't get to slide, saying or doing things that either make you uncomfortable or offend you, and so forth. While writing this book, I was speaking with a potential client within a company for which I had already conducted work. I told her that I preferred to have my name listed as Dr. Indigo when I presented. She went on to explain why she would not honor that request. She threw out that it was based on policy; however, someone else in the company stated that such wasn't a problem or a policy. I hate it when people do things and hide behind policy, like a kid throwing a rock at you and then hiding behind a tree as if you won't know that a rock was thrown. I explained to her that I don't use my last name, and that Dr. Indigo is my brand. I went on to explain that most people don't know Dr. Phil's or Dr. Oz's last name. She guffawed! If she had coffee in her mouth, I'm sure she would have spit it out, as she condescendingly said, "They are celebrities. You aren't a celebrity." I retorted, "First of all, they weren't always celebrities. Secondly, I never said that I was a celebrity." I went on to say that when I spoke at an international conference with well over 1,000 women in the audience, a prominent woman contacted me and said, "Dr. Indigo, a hospital where I sit on the board is having a fundraiser and needs a celebrity to host the evening. You are a celebrity! ...Will you host our annual fundraising event?" I didn't call myself a celebrity, but she watched how people responded to me as I left the stage and could not leave the room for an hour as people wanted autographs, pictures and to shake my hand and chat. So, I pushed back and said, "To some, I am a celebrity but that is not the point. This is about honoring my request." And, I told her that she offended me. I spoke my truth, not her truth. She neither had the right nor the permission to tell me what I am or am not. Don't allow people to define you! Speak your truth. As an oh by the way, a week later, when we presented in a studio with lights and cameras, her client said, "Oh, you two look like celebrities." I thanked her client and looked over at lil miss and she deflected the compliment, which is a statement of how she probably doesn't see her own worth.

26. No Response is a Response

I always believed that it was a professional courtesy to acknowledge everyone's message when I received an email. I believed that not sending any type of response was confusing and rude. I would tell my employees even if you are unable to give an answer, please let me know that you, at a minimum, received my message. But, as I start encountering a world where everything is posted, law suits are common practice and people often misinterpret and archive anything that you say, maybe no response is a better response. It can be as a loud as the spoken word. But, don't allow this to be your go-to stance as a way of avoiding conflict when something needs to be addressed.

27. Feedback is a Gift

The other day, I read an email message that took me aback. I hit reply and typed a very direct and factual response that served as feedback. In short, I'd partnered with an organization; wherein, the lead person, who was fairly new, was my point of contact. I made suggestions and advised her on things that I knew would be in our best interest. She made it clear that it was 'their' client and she knew what they wanted: thus, I followed her lead as a subcontractor. They didn't get the contract, and the feedback from the potential client on why they didn't win the contract was exactly what I suggested to her. I wrote a statement that said, "If you recall..." Before hitting send, I let the email sit overnight and decided that I wouldn't respond at all. I thought that there was absolutely nothing positive that would come from pointing out her failure. This is where no response could have been a response. But, it would have been disingenuous to not say something in response to her email. I also believed that this could be a lesson learned or a teachable moment. After letting the revisions sit overnight, I bounced it off a trusted colleague, tweaked it to be less emotional, and I sent the message. It created space to discuss future collaborations with rules of engagement. If I didn't say something, I would have been confronted with the same issue down the road, and it's very difficult to attempt to remind people of things once the wind blows over. Feedback must be within the same timeframe of the infraction.

28. Time is of the Essence

I used to quickly respond to people as if a clock were ticking and I owed an answer to everyone about everything, immediately. No. You don't owe anyone an immediate response. Time is of the essence, so allow it to work on your behalf. As a kid, my parents would require that we (my brother and I) answer quickly when they asked a question of us. They would ask the question and stare at us, which was intimidating, and we felt pressured to answer, even if we didn't know the answer. That carried over for me when I was in the military, especially during boot camp inspections. A Drill Instructor would ask a question, stare at me and demand an immediate answer. But, unlike my parents, what they taught me is that when I didn't know something, then I was to say, "Ma'am private Triplett does not know, but by 1300 I will have the answer for the sergeant, ma'am." What I want you to understand is that if you don't know, hell, you don't know so don't make up something. Just answer by letting whomever is asking the question of you know that you are not exactly sure of something and if she gives you a little time, you can provide the correct answer. There is no shame in not knowing, but rather not knowing and giving an incorrect answer is shameful.

29. Be You

I spoke of this in the second book by using Y.O.U. as an acronym for Years of Understanding. You should possess as much knowledge about yourself to be the you that you want to be. Recently, I was teaching an Authentic Leadership course for executives. Mid-way through the course, participants were concerned that they weren't being genuine or authentic if they changed, which was the foundation of the session. I explained the importance of situational judgement and asked them to lean into the course and trust the process. At the conclusion, I showed a slide with the picture of a candle, the first light bulb, and the progressive upgrade of light bulbs to LED. I gave the story that I believe that if we are light, then we can be candles all the way to LEDs. At one time, the candlestick maker said that his invention will always be necessary because people needed the light to read well into the night. But, today we don't use candles to light our home. We have every kind of light bulb imaginable. That doesn't mean that the candle is obsolete. We still buy candles for different uses. In short, the source of light has changed and what we do with lights have changed, but we still need light. You will change and should change, or you will become obsolete. As the game changes, you must adjust; that is career maturity. Be you but don't get stuck in being someone that is unwilling to grow, change or transform into someone better.

30. And, Cut! That's a Wrap

Similar to a movie director completing a scene, I too must wrap this up. "And, cut! That's a wrap," was a phrase that I said in meetings, interviews and nearly anything that I had to stop abruptly. It would often sound rude, but there are times when you realize that someone isn't taking a breath to let you get a word in, that whatever someone is saying is taking way too long to say, or that the conversation is too far off track. I would do a hand gesture by clapping my hands together and saying, "And, cut! That's a wrap." You need to know when enough is enough. I don't allow people to hijack my conversation or time, and you will be less frustrated when you do the same. So, this is where I stop. I could continue to write and never finish this book, but that wouldn't serve anyone, at this point.

In closing, I thoroughly enjoyed sharing my journey and giving you tools and guidance that will support you in your career journey. So, when all has been said, it's time to wrap up, yeah? A scene can drag out and the audience will become bored. So, I will finish this scene, i.e. this book and move to the next scene. I am already starting to write the next book, but I have to complete this book, where I have found healing and comfort through sharing. Thank you for reading the *Playing by the Unwritten Rules* three-part book series. It has been a delight to share this personal space with people all around the world, and I hope that you will have immense success from my insights.

Similar to thinking that the movie is over and walking out during the credits, you turn back around to the screen because the Director slipped in a whole new scene. Here's the hidden scene. I will finish with the beginning. I stated in the Introduction that change and transformation are the most precious journeys. If you read all three books, I am confident that you will experience profound success by adopting and implementing the techniques or concepts that I have shared. Whoever you are, or are becoming, embrace it, own it and run with it. And, most of all, have fun being you on whatever path you decide to take. And, above all, play the game by the unwritten rules. Lastly, my current closing statement, 'With pure intentions and purposefulness I share my story and journey with you'.

The End For Now